e to be returned on or befor
the last date below.

pull back to ½
(short from out

candid as possible

testing of turntable

~light on wire   (this is on a table top)

~ light orbit

as ~ wall throng activity;

Construction

BG drops to
non represent
3d moment

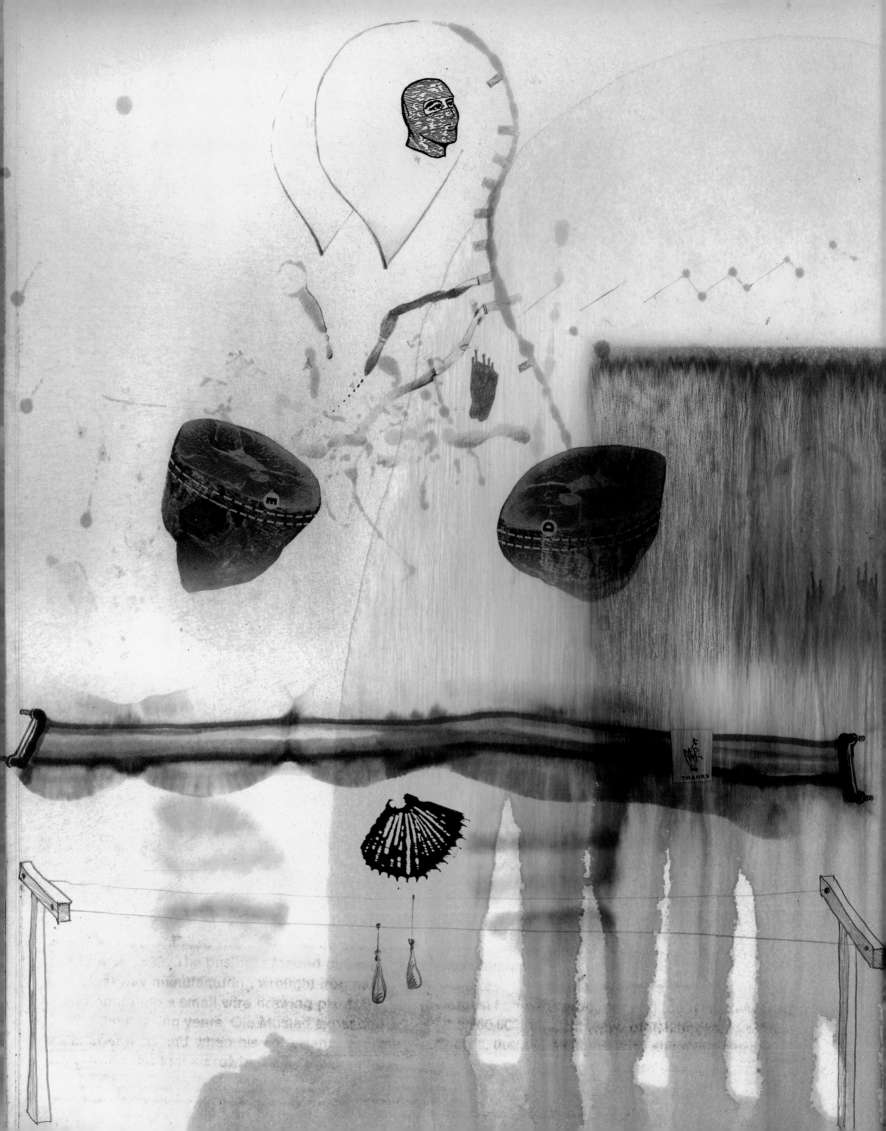

schools, and accustomed to lower large number of persons
dominant feeling of particular creeds
and where well as heating is
expressed by means of
the lighting,
cases of heating buildings by the
vent light aspirating utilized. is dispensed with, the
vent stack being inside of it, the
requiring the use of direct-lighting
smoke flue , all the way to the top,
not that the light source cannot be
being made of heavy boiler plate. The chief trouble
comfortable. Large
the naturally be gravity, system of
high-powered, weather is a unit may but little
to produce at the same time that is just as necessary
produce a high standard without
as in severe weather; the age
lighting its many forms in those
of the fan, which do not have the air in the orna stack is
ments, domes, the difference and other features of the
air inside and that outside in a manner that it shows the
fire must be kept parts to be modeled i mild
an in cold weather, in very well. concealed
above the capital and s
using a fan. worthy of used instead
to produce the other movement
but brighter is seldom in the conditions exist
that preclude the suitable high
units behind the chancel or the light
the altar concealed behind
the ceremonial uses of light should
not be overlooked. COMBINATION

The combination warming is
24. Church-Window Lighting. not all from the part of a building,
beauty of large night
illuminating these the same building warmed by
water very pleasing night from a heater other
hand, The air with view of people warms the
rooms they may be those remote one or more
so projectors inside the church. run to the
through the colored glass good draft, warmed by
radiators

then bitterish. Me., S. and W.

globular ; seed at first sweet,
then bitterish.

smooth ; bitter.

MYRICACEÆ, THE GALE FAMILY.

Shrubs with resinous-dotted often fragrant simple leaves, and inconspicuous flowers solitary under a scale-like bract, both kinds in short catkins or heads, and destitute of any proper calyx or corolla; the 1-seeded fruit a fleshy little drupe or small nut dry and commonly coated with wax.

ing 2 slender stigmas.

MYRICA, BAYBERRY, WAX-MYRTLE. some sweetish shrubs.

M. Gale, Sweet Gale. Gold-bogs N.; with pale wedge-lanceolate leaves, rather toothed above, crowded, and as if winged by a pair of scales.

M. cerifera, Bayberry, Wax-Myrtle. coast, Canada.... becoming waxy white berries. scattered thorny grey berries and appearing like berries.

M. asplenifolia, Eng. to fid. leaves, pinnatifid and sweet-aromatic.

CUPULIFERÆ, THE OAK FAMILY.

These are shrubs with alternate and simple straight-veined leaves, deciduous stipules, and monoecious flowers, the sterile in catkins (except in the Beech) either sterile solitary or clustered spikes and furnished with an involucre which becomes 1-celled 1-seeded nut or in Birches and Alders within a more or less rounded,

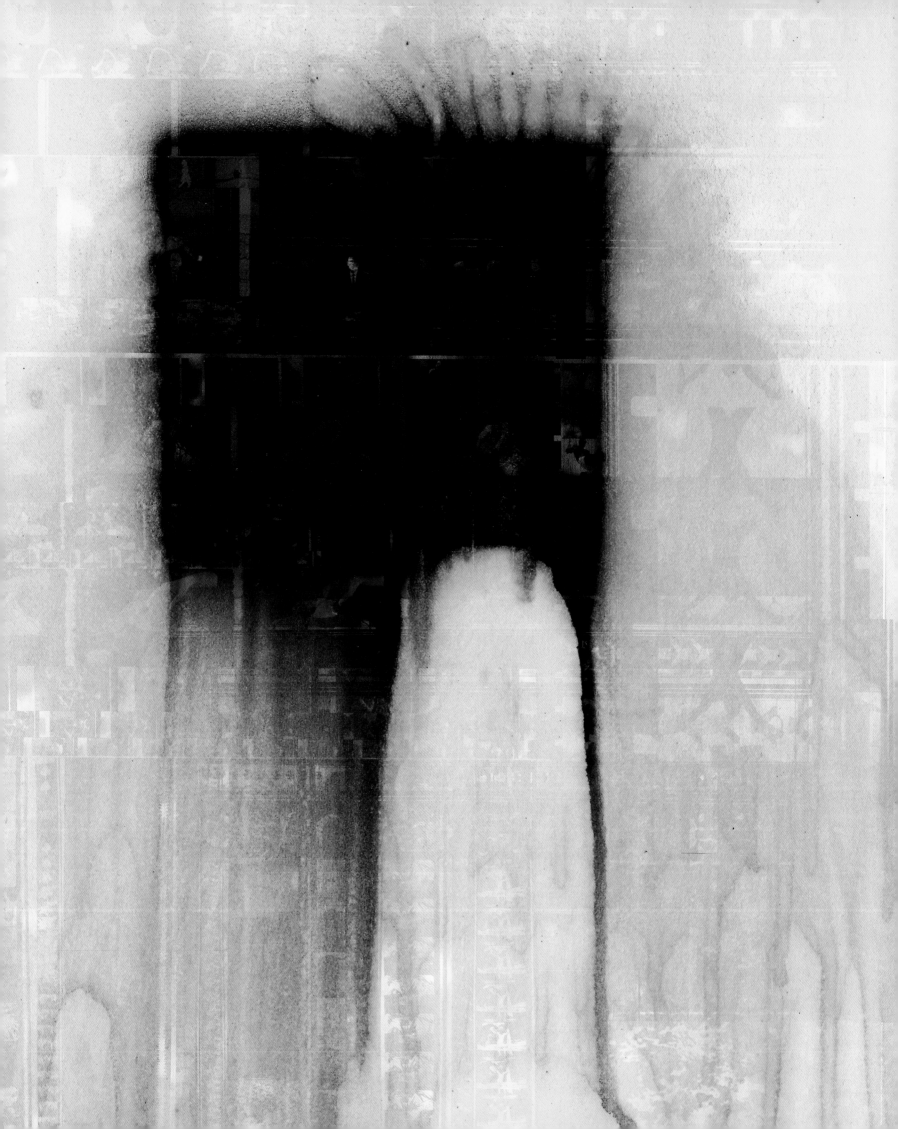

Pat O'Neill:

Views From Lookout Mountain

Santa Monica Museum of Art
Bergamot Station G1
2525 Michigan Avenue
Santa Monica, CA 90402
T. 310 586 6488
F. 310 586 6487
www.smmoa.org

Steidl Verlag
Düstere Strasse 4
D-37073 Göttingen
Germany
T. +49 551 49 60 60
F. +49 551 49 60 649
e-mail: mail@steidl.de
www.steidl.de

First published in 2004
by the Santa Monica Museum of Art,
Bergamot Station 2525 Michigan Avenue,
Building G1 Santa Monica, CA 90402
and Steidl Verlag, Düstere Strasse 4,
D-37073 Göttingen, Germany,
in conjunction with the exhibition
Pat O'Neill: Views from Lookout Mountain.

EXHIBITION ITINERARY

Santa Monica Museum of Art
September 11–November 13, 2004

Cornerhouse, Manchester, England

ISBN 3-86521-021-X

Editor: Stephanie Emerson
Designer: Michael Worthington
Assistant Designer: Meina Co
Printer: Steidl, Göttingen, Germany

Printed and bound in Germany

Pat O'Neill: Views from Lookout Mountain

Julie Lazar

Contributions by
Paul Arthur
John G. Hanhardt
Howard Singerman
Erika Suderburg

Collaborative Project by
Pat O'Neill &
Michael Worthington

SANTA MONICA MUSEUM OF ART
STEIDL VERLAG

CONTENTS

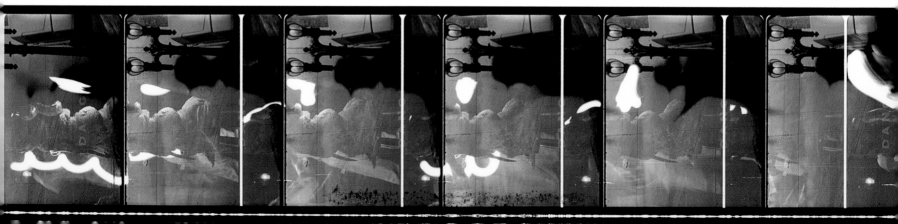

FOREWORD
BY ELSA LONGHAUSER
EXECUTIVE DIRECTOR, SANTA MONICA MUSEUM OF ART

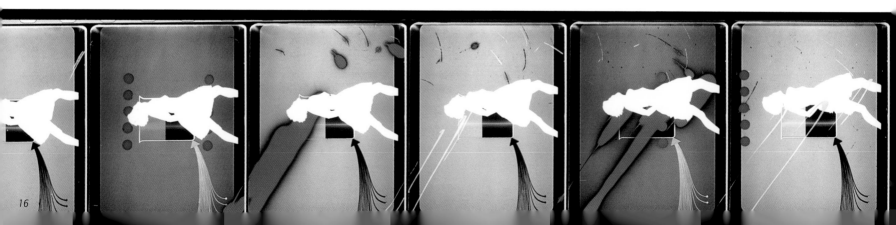

Pat O'Neill is a filmmaker's filmmaker, an artist's artist. His name elicits reverent praise across generations, and yet, as is often the case, his work is not widely known. The Santa Monica Museum of Art is pleased, therefore, to present *Pat O'Neill: Views from Lookout Mountain*, the first major exhibition and publication to examine this important artist's forty-year career.

O'Neill's particular hybrid aesthetic is revealed in work that includes a variety of genres—film projection, drawing, sculpture, photography, installation, and interactive DVD-ROM. The process and dimension of his production is meticulously examined in this book through the scholarly perspectives of art historians Paul Arthur, Howard Singerman, and Erika Suderburg and curators John Hanhardt and Julie Lazar.

Guest curator Julie Lazar has worked with confidence and devotion to organize every aspect of this endeavor. *Pat O'Neill: Views from Lookout Mountain* marks the most recent addition to her distinguished roster of innovative curatorial work. Many others have also given generous and heartfelt support; I would like to add my voice to Julie Lazar's and Pat O'Neill's in thanking all those whose diligence and commitment have given this landmark project enduring definition and form.

After opening in Santa Monica, a retrospective of O'Neill's films will be shown at the Solomon R. Guggenheim Museum in New York. The exhibition will then travel to the Cornerhouse in Manchester, England. In keeping with its mission to explore and proclaim the rich artistic legacy of Los Angeles, Santa Monica Museum of Art welcomes the opportunity to add this prodigious body of work to the art historical canon.

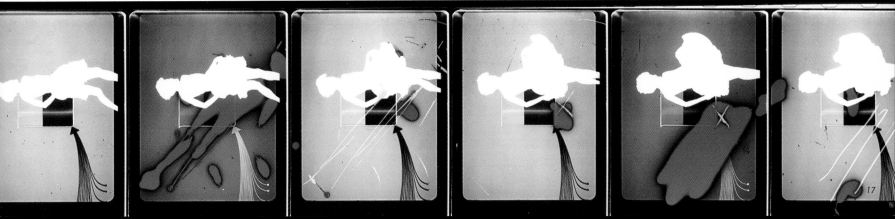

INTRODUCTION
BY JULIE LAZAR

We have built in our country
the greatest capability the world has ever seen
for the manufacture and fabrication of useful products.
But the appetite of our factories and industrial plants
for raw materials is enormous, and the hunger for raw materials
grows as technology and consumer demand keep creating
new products and new processes.

What makes the electrons, or whatever they are called,
come together and form the shape of the picture?
That's what I don't understand.

Good. Let's add that: what... makes... the shape...
or pattern of the picture.
Is there anything else? Well then, let's see the film.
Don, will you close the shades?

—Dialogue from *Trouble in the Image,* 1996

When he was seventy years old, Marcel Duchamp suggested that, "The spectator brings the work [of art] in contact with the external world by deciphering and interpreting its inner qualification and thus adding his contribution to the creative act."[1] *Pat O'Neill: Views from Lookout Mountain* affords the public its first opportunity to see a selection of distinctive visual art made by Pat O'Neill from 1961 through 2004, along with a retrospective of his distinguished films.

During the early 1940s, when Pat O'Neill was still a boy, one of the primary sources of entertainment for young children was the stories their parents read aloud to them during moments set aside from the demands of the day. Another source was comic books, whose graphic format was developed at that time, along with invention of about 400 superhero characters.[2] Instead of being totally absorbed in electronic, interactive playstations and computers like today's youth, kids were engrossed in the texts and illustrated picture books found in libraries or in magazines acquired from the local newsstand. The extra-large photographs in *Life Magazine*'s glossy pages changed how people in the U.S. perceived and interpreted the magnitude of national and world events each week.

Around 1946, the raging growth of television's popularity increased the opportunities for image proliferation and distribution through "mass media" exponentially. The burgeoning communications industry flooded poor quality, black-and-white electronic pictures with monophonic sounds into the living rooms of most middle-class Americans (color was introduced later in 1949). TV audiences were fed a daily diet of commercial advertisements, newsroom renditions of reality, and a steady progression of sometimes wacky, other times rewarding, but always entertaining programs. Instead of functioning as a passive piece of household furniture, this one-directional message pipeline became an overtly persuasive, formative presence in the home.

Only Hollywood movies projected onto big screens in glamorous theaters could compete for the public's attention and imagination. A mere sixty years later, global communications industries have stimulated the broad proliferation of personal computers, cell phones, cable and satellite broadcasts, interactive televisions, and wireless handheld devices used by the public to access a world of information.

Now it is possible for individuals in first- and many third-world countries to be in constant communication with one another. People with average incomes can afford to transport tiny digital computers on their person to just about any location on the planet and gain access to thousands of channels and multi-millions of websites at any time day or night. Through the convergence of disparate media in recent history, it is possible to witness first-hand how use of these tools has come into play and affected seismic shifts in the socio-political conditions of places like China, Kosovo, Chiapas, the Philippines, and the U.S.

Screens are ubiquitous in contemporary culture. Indeed, the American Film Institute recently established a Screen Education Department solely devoted to increasing the screen literacy levels of public elementary students across Los Angeles County. To those who are on the cutting edge of media theory, Marshall McLuhan's ideas might seem old hat but to the layperson, they remain prescient:

Today, in the electronic age of instantaneous communication, I believe that our survival, and at the very least our comfort and happiness, is predicated on understanding the nature of our new environment, because unlike previous environmental changes, the electric media constitute a total and near-instantaneous transformation of culture, values and attitude.

1. Marcel Duchamp, "The Creative Act." *Aspen* no. 5 + 6, item 13. (1957) http://www.ubu.com/aspen/aspen5and6/audio5E.html
2. Rafael de Viveiros Lima, "Some History (so far...)," http://www.geocities.com/SoHo/5537/hist.htm.

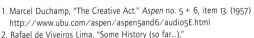
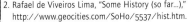

He continues:

The content or message of any particular medium has about as much importance as the stenciling on the casing of an atomic bomb. But the ability to perceive media-induced extensions of man, once the province of the artist, is now being expanded as the new environment of electric information makes possible a new degree of perception and critical awareness by non-artists.[3]

The insidious influence of corporate image production and dissemination upon twenty-first-century world cultures is present in the background of this exhibition like visual white noise. In the foreground are the creative ideas, objects, and images of a single artist from Los Angeles. In his studio on Lookout Mountain, Pat O'Neill has created a body of art work over four decades that melds different artistic disciplines into complex combinations of media, materials, and slices of time that are remarkably compelling to those fortunate to make their discovery.

Like other Los Angeles-based artists of his generation (particularly those affiliated with the Ferus Gallery), Pat O'Neill loves cars. At age eighteen, he even designed and built a fiberglass sports car as a functioning prototype. He enrolled at UCLA in the Department of Fine Art, initially specializing in Industrial and Graphic Design. After Robert Heinecken lobbied and negotiated for photography to be recognized as one of the disciplines in the Fine Arts program with official sanction as an area of proper investigation within the university, O'Neill transferred there and became Heinecken's graduate student and teaching assistant. "In those days, there was a very clear line between working in the commercial culture and working in the fine arts,"[4] his wife, art historian Beverly O'Neill, explained.

The O'Neills met in the early 1960s at UCLA in the university's first film history class, taught by Hugh Gray. Gray brought interesting people to class like Josef von Sternberg, Otto Preminger, and Fatty Arbuckle's wife. He introduced students to the experimental films of Dziga Vertov and Serge Eisenstein. "Pat was going to experimental screenings at the Coronet Theater on La Cienega. He knew about the films of Luis Buñuel, Len Lye, and Normen McLaren." At the time, Beverly O'Neill worked as a grading assistant for Mary Holmes who was one of few women professors at the school. "Pat would leave off photographs on my desk of decapitated baby dolls, decimated oil rigs, things that had been on fire and the residue of it all. They were very exotic for their time." She recalled that, "After he finished his MFA, Pat decided that he absolutely did not want to be a commercial artist. He would be willing to do technical work in the commercial world but he would never be willing to sell his ideas to it. He would not invest in that way."

"Pat's whole idea in making 3-D forms came out of making cars," Beverly surmised. In his own estimate, he was "a cracker-jack model maker," with a serious habit of "salvaging industrial waste and making assemblages from found pieces—mostly metal objects; some had moveable parts that responded to balance." Crushed cars, abandoned spray-painted vehicles, corroding auto parts, vintage models; they often figure into his photographs, films, and inkjet prints. "He began to make those fiberglass shaped pieces with highly polished surfaces," Beverly explained, "somewhere between using an industrial technique and an odd kind of biomorphism. He wondered what it would be like if they were represented in motion by being translated into film. That's when he did [the film] *7362* (1967)."

3. Marshall McLuhan, "The Playboy Interview: Marshall McLuhan," (March 1969), http://www.nephridium.org/features/indymedia/mcluhan_interview.html
4. Interview with Beverly O'Neill, November 6, 2003. All quotes attributed to Beverly O'Neill are from this interview.

In his interview with O'Neill curator John G. Hanhardt follows up: "So something important synthesized around *7362*. Bilateral splitting is an image-processing technique. But you were also interested in the philosophic and materialist notion of the object, which is complicated by this process of doubling. I am fascinated by the connections you have suggested between image, sculpture, and film. Through processing you seem to have imbued film with tactility."[5]

Years later, Pat O'Neill formed Lookout Mountain Films, a special effects company, in order to support his art production. He and Beverly spent the better part of thirty years living on Lookout Mountain Avenue in Laurel Canyon and only recently moved to Pasadena where he is building a new studio. "Curiously, there was another Lookout Mountain film unit that had closed the year before we moved [to Laurel Canyon]," he mentioned to John Hanhardt in passing. "It was actually an Air Force base up at the top of the hill where some five hundred people were employed making films for the government. They did all the government documents of nuclear tests; all the films that the Navy, Air Force, and NASA used as documents for Congress, for training and for public release. It is a wonderful underground facility with five stories cut down into granite. It has been empty since '68. As it turns out, Oskar Fischinger lived just a quarter of a mile on the other side of that."

Art historian, Howard Singerman thoughtfully examines the artist's photographs, sculptures, drawings, and prints in his essay, taking into account the interplay between the strategies of O'Neill's early collages and his films:

> The collages are not matted or backed, but suspended, sandwiched between two panes of glass, a reference not only to windows but to the "gate" of a camera or projector or an optical printer, open to light on

either side. Where O'Neill's film work often suggests the influence and presence of still photography, these heavily framed collages seems the inverse, an attempt to put film at the center of a studio practice in a way that would reference both the artisanal making of the sculpture and the hand processing of film.

Film historian David E. James sees in Pat O'Neill's work, "connections with the industry and industrial kinds of production on the one hand and the aesthetic sensibility that's associated with the avant-garde on the other." "That seems to be a very powerful thing." O'Neill agrees that, "the illusion and the denial of the illusion, are both present at the same time. For example, opaque black mattes, film used to hide part of an image so as to replace it with another, have a fascination that comes from their incomplete descriptiveness. The edges of shapes are hauntingly photographic, yet their center is vacant and flat. Characters are both knowable and invisible. [Optical printing] is a technology particular to a very specialized craft, which I am re-using, if you will, in the spirit of collage."[6]

Leading film critic and historian Paul Arthur observes in his essay that, "A master trope involving the film image as simultaneous oasis and mirage surfaces frequently in O'Neill's work." About his highly respected 1989 film, *Water and Power*, Arthur goes on to say that:

> Within a complex calculus of elemental and man-made properties, O'Neill positions cinema alongside water, heat, and land as aspects of a single ecological system, in which technology is neither inevitably hostile nor naively redemptive. In this fashion fixed formal, symbolic, and topographic oppositions can start to bend and interpenetrate: abstract animation versus straight photography, interior versus exterior; industry versus culture; desert versus city.

5. Interview with Pat O'Neill, March 1, 2003.

6. David E. James, "An Interview with Pat O'Neill," http://mfj-online.org/journalPages/MFJ30,31/DJamesInterview.html (Fall 1997).

Snake is on the Right, a screen-sized composite inkjet print completed in 2003, encapsulates the artist's fascination with the languages of graphic art, photography and film—and is especially related to techniques the filmmaker employed in making *Trouble in the Image* from 1996:

> It consists of two panels of more or less equal size. Laid over these is a screen of linear frames that were taken from an optical house's wipe chart. This is a list of all the various ways one can break up a screen to make an animated transition from one shot to another. Lynwood Dunn and others developed this methodology in the thirties. The two panels contain line cuts: illustrations from a 1907 German Zoology text and from Ridpath's Universal History *(1899). I liked the way the checkered skin of the snake talks to the geometric shapes of the wipes, and the way the curvilinear snake echoes the drapery in the left panel. Laid over all of this are softly defined shapes made by scratching into opaque film, then photographing light passing through the marks. The wipe chart, with its seemingly hieroglyphic ranks and files, partially obscures the line drawings, and is in turn obscured by the cursive marking. The four elements in the composition were brought into a kind of fragile balance of oppositions.*

Pat O'Neill is a disciplined, obsessively hard worker when it comes to making art. It took almost ten years to complete his film, *The Decay of Fiction* (2002), for example. Nearly a year and a half of that time was spent recording the interplay of shadows and the changing available light pouring into rooms, down corridors, through passageways, and lapping over the deteriorating paraphernalia of the historic Ambassador Hotel. "[*The Decay of Fiction*] is about illusion, the institution that thrives on creating illusions for other people... it's basically about placing narratives into a documentary space and keeping the two intact."[7] Later, he used

source materials culled from the film to create a separate ("performance") series of composite prints that he refers to as single frame movies:

> When you look at an image, your experience of it may not be of it as a whole: Rather, you explore it sequentially—the artist gives you a place to enter a work of art and suggestions about how to move through its spaces. This movement has a particular style, pace, and destination, and could be said to be a sequence of events or an unfolding of perceptions over time.[8]

Pat O'Neill formed his ideas and skills in the heat of the Vietnam War era and is refining them still during the present War on Terror. It would be a mistake to see him as a "political artist," but it would be equally misguided not to understand that he pays very close attention to what is going on in the world. The present U.S. administration exploits all possible methods of communication in a concurrent battle especially familiar to those who lived through both the nightmarish propaganda of World War II and the conservative backlash that brought with it harsh restraints imposed upon freedom of expression during the 1950s. Who can fully comprehend the impact of the current power struggle over the control, content, and flow of images that depict or mask actions being conducted in the name of American democracy throughout the world? The future and present require that audiences make clear-minded, intelligent assessments of what is being conveyed by these media "massages." What are the cultural, economic, social, and political effects that these expressions are having on the world's populations, including here in the U.S.? Artists may not supply answers to these questions, but they do increase the public understanding of how mechanical reproduction, temporality, and media impact perception. This is especially evident in art made since the early twentieth century by employing techniques or through movements like Futurism (Malevich),

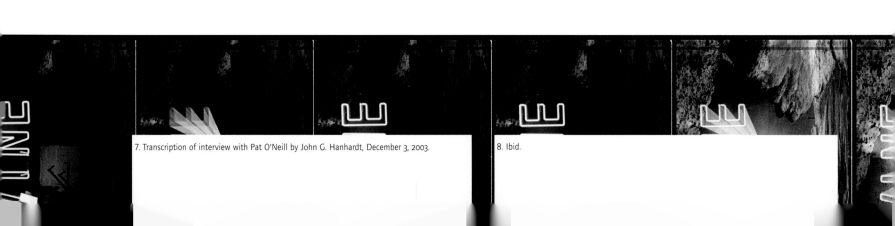

7. Transcription of interview with Pat O'Neill by John G. Hanhardt, December 3, 2003.

8. Ibid.

montage (Eisenstein), Dadaism (Duchamp), Surrealism (Man Ray, Dalí),
collage (Cornell), modernism (Picasso, Reinhardt, Caro), and more recently
in Pop (Warhol, Rauschenberg, Rosenquist, Ruscha, Hamilton, Bengston),
Fluxus (Cage, Maciunus), assemblage (Kienholz, Conner), Structuralism
(Snow), Minimalism (LeWitt, Judd, Serra), Beat (Berman, Jess), Conceptualism
(Huebler, Baldessari), New Cinema (Deren, Brakhage, Whitney brothers),
postmodernism (Haacke, Gober, Koons), and contemporary art (Turrell,
Lockhart).

Artists' contributions are so meaningful because their works are imbued
with the value of creativity as opposed to the dogma of corporate
consumerism or the coerciveness of political postulation. As Duchamp said,
in order to complete the creative process the spectator adds his or her
contribution to the creative act. Art reinforces the importance of dialogue
sorely lacking in mass communication and helps to define why it has been
so important to humanity throughout recorded history. In her perceptive
contribution to this book, artist Erika Suderburg sums up why Pat O'Neill's
vibrant work is so meaningful: "He deploys co-existing stratas of obsolescence, repose, revolution, consumption, and anarchic agitation. Ultimately
he engages us in seeing."

Jack decides to take a quick trip down to the airport   Jack decides to take a quick trip down to the airport   Jack decides to

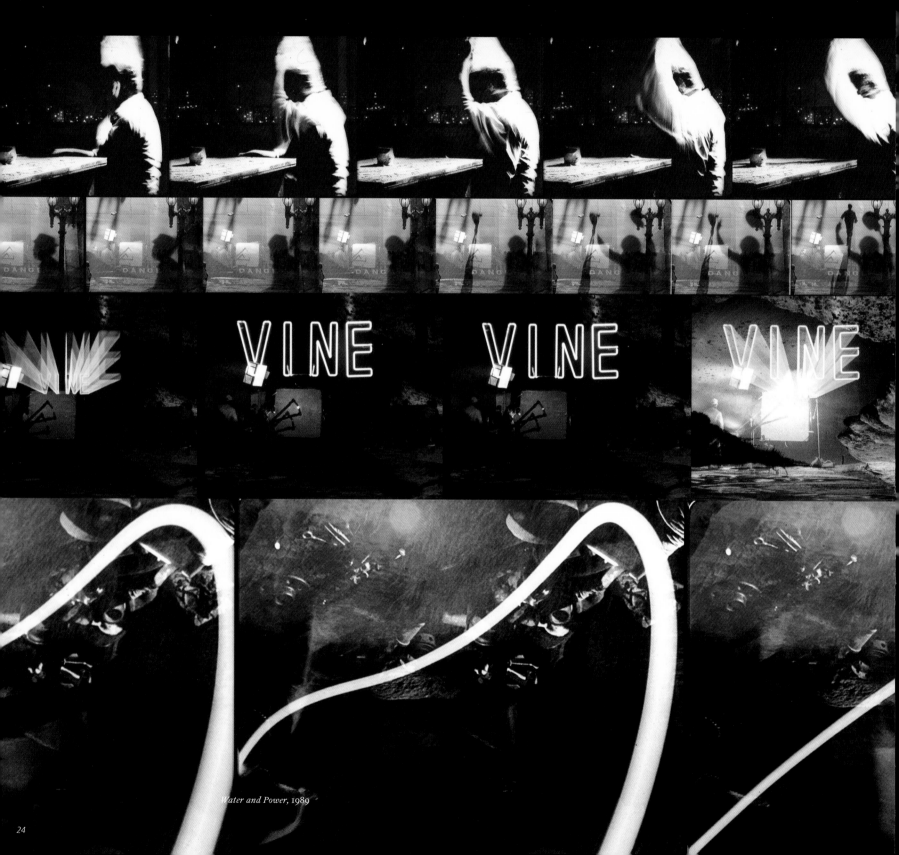

Water and Power, 1989

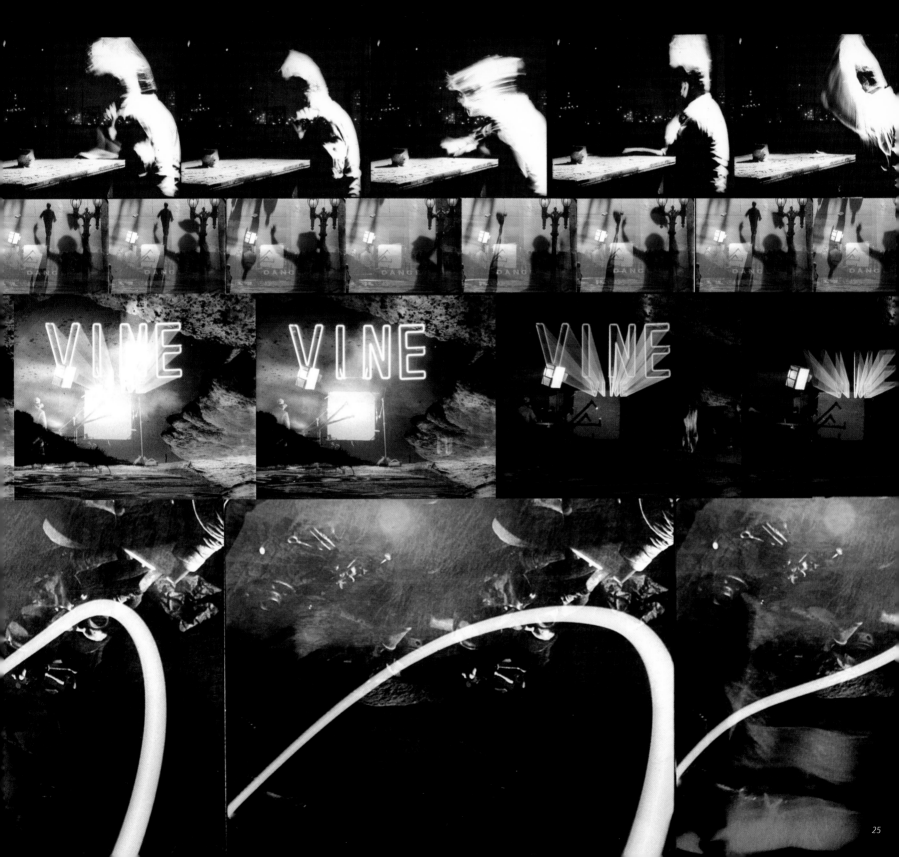

Untitled (Collage 1), 1965

Untitled (Collage 2), 1965

Atlantic Auto Wrecking Series (1), 1961

TOP (CLOCKWISE): *Atlantic Auto Wrecking Series (2)*, 1961; *Atlantic Auto Wrecking Series (4)*, 1961;
Atlantic Auto Wrecking Series (3), 1961

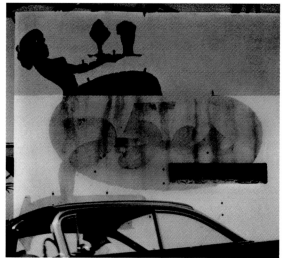

TOP: *Untitled (Fun)*, 1963
BOTTOM: *Untitled (25er)*, 1965

TOP: *Untitled (Downtown, LA Series 2)*, 1961
BOTTOM: *Untitled (Downtown, LA Series 1)*, 1961

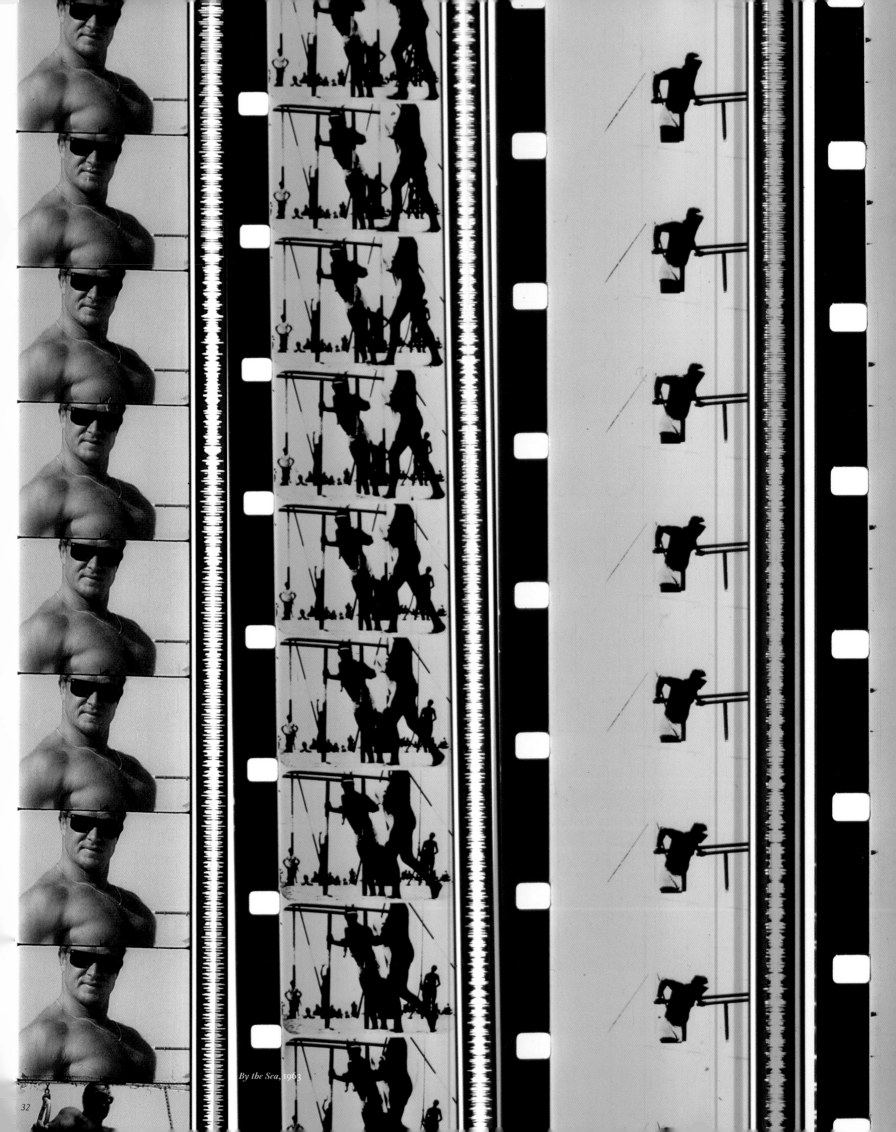

By the Sea, 1963

32

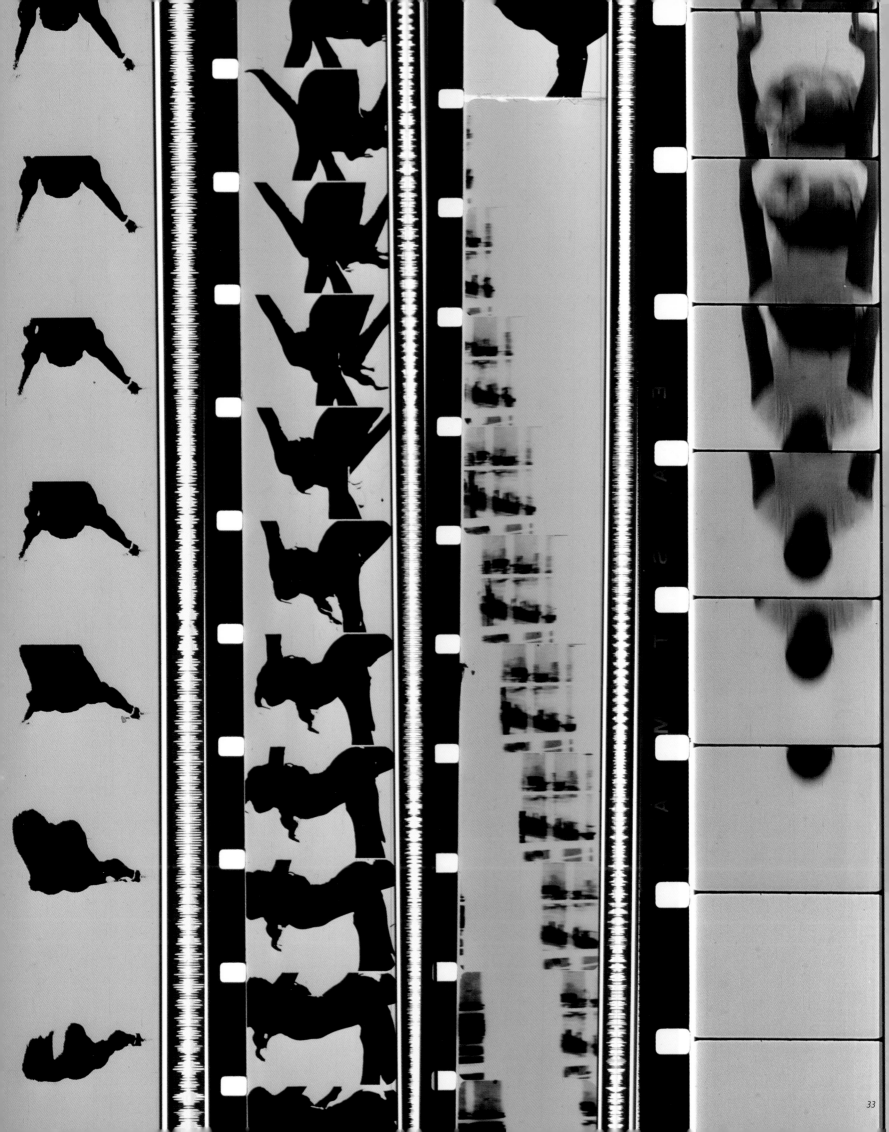

Rocky Grant, Windows, 2002

A Pair of Bones, 2003

Untitled (3), 1994

Sweet Pea, 2002

Screen was presented on a rear-projection screen set into a square opening in a dark-ened gallery wall. The three-minute loop consists of polychrome imagery derived from spray-painted, clear, 16mm leader. The leader is first printed on black-and-white film and then onto color film using color filters. The piece explores a series of ideas for obtaining mixture of color in the eye. The apparent animation of dots is random.

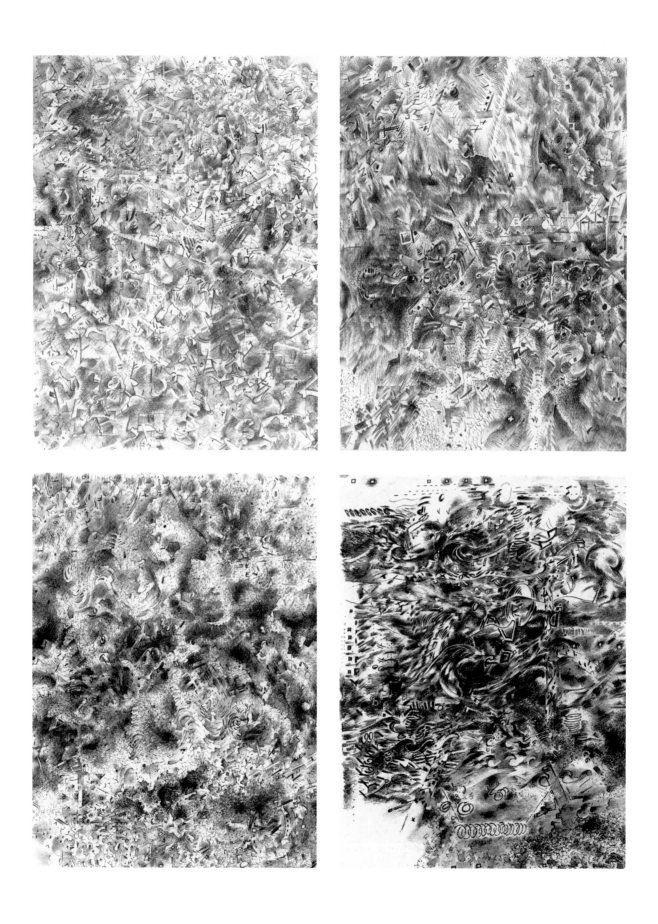

FROM TOP LEFT, CLOCKWISE: *Untitled*, 1984; *Untitled*, 1985;
Untitled (1), 1994; *Untitled*, 1986

Untitled (5), 1994

8-22-94

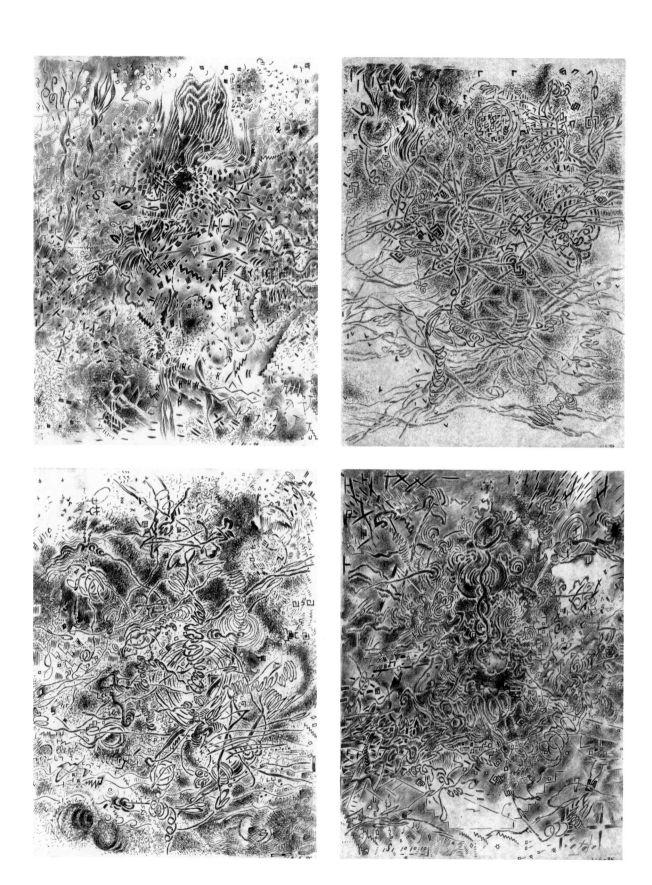

FROM TOP LEFT, CLOCKWISE: *Untitled (2)*, 1994; *Untitled (4)*, 1994; *Untitled (3)*, 1995, collection
of Gaby and Wilhelm Schuermann, Herzogenrath, Germany; *Untitled (1)*, 1995

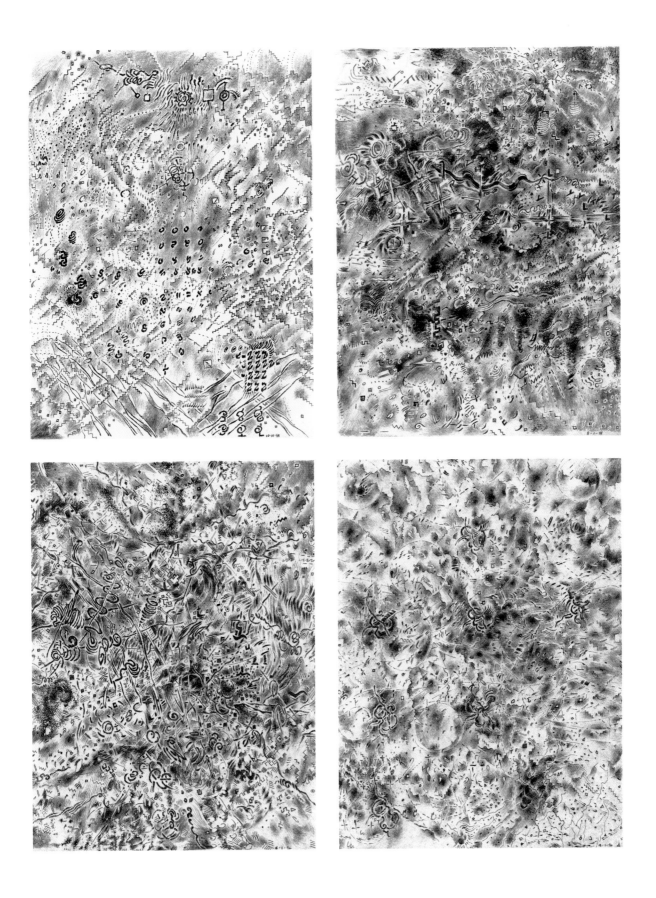

FROM TOP LEFT, CLOCKWISE: *Untitled (1)*, 1996; *Untitled (2)*, 1996;
Untitled (4), 1996; *Untitled (3)*, 1996

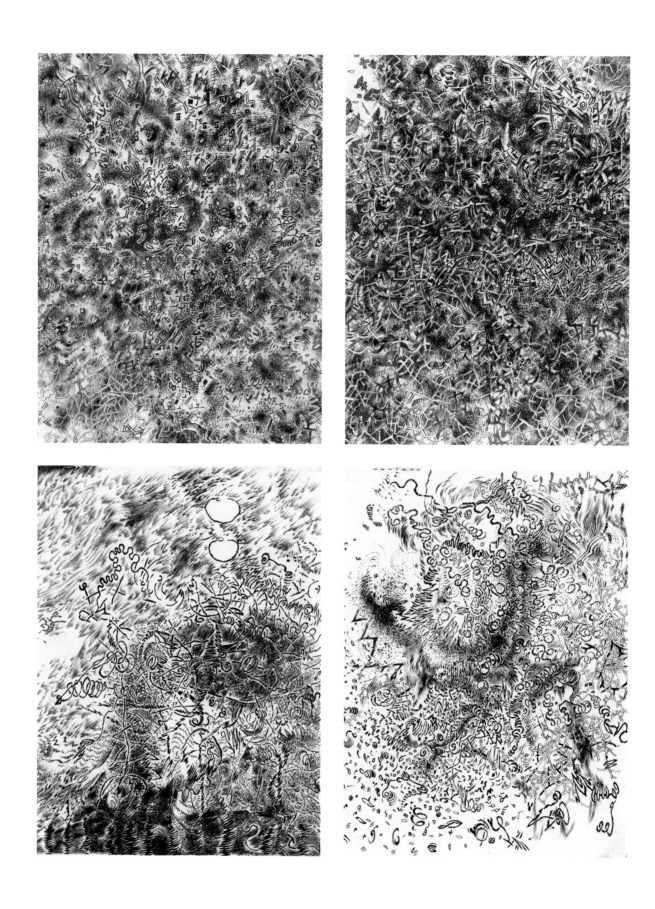

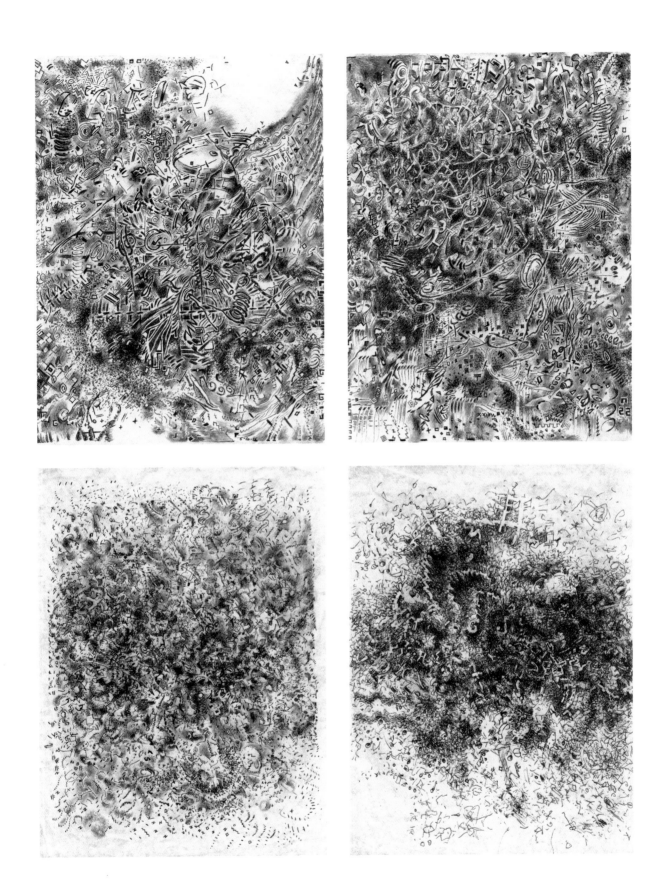

FROM TOP LEFT, CLOCKWISE: *Untitled (1)*, 2001; *Untitled (2)*, 2001;
Untitled (4), 2001; *Untitled (3)*, 2001

Untitled (2), 1995

Untitled (Horn), 2003

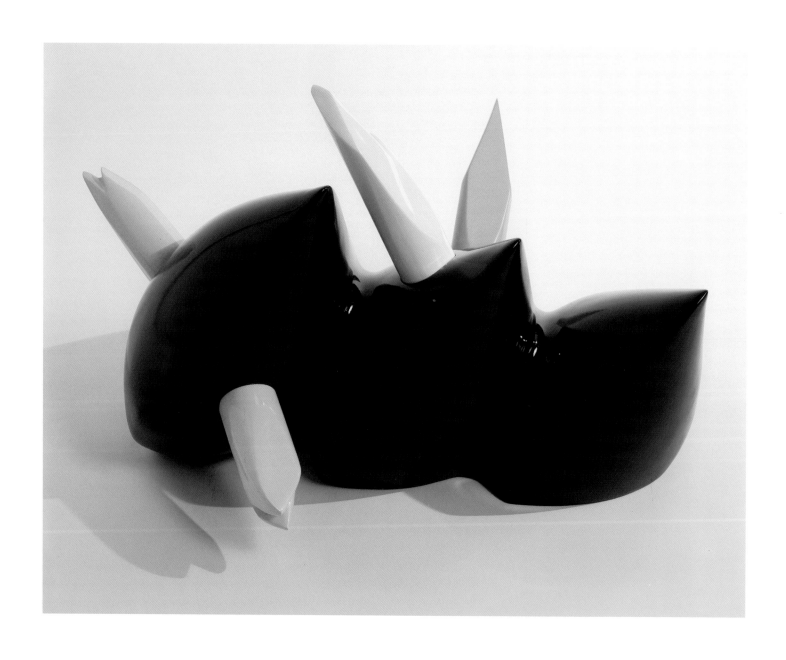

Bill 'n Bob at the Lab, 2003

Snake is on the Right, 2003

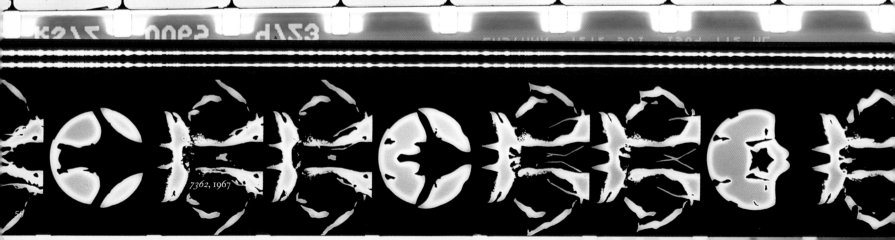

7362, 1967

Untitled (Dingo 4), 1980

 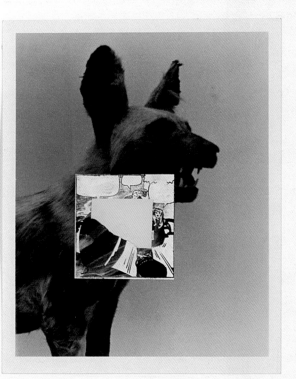

Untitled (Dingo 3), 1980

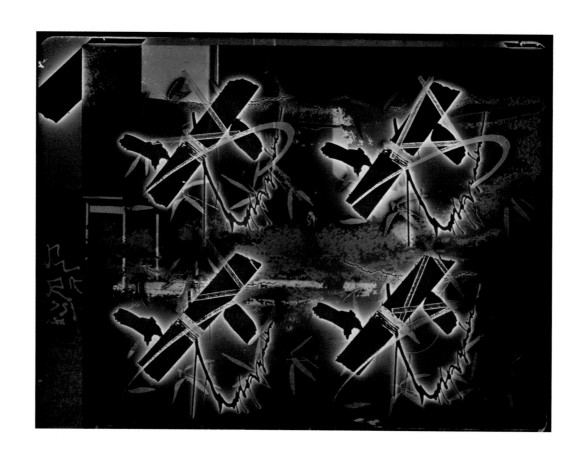

Punch Me In, 1984

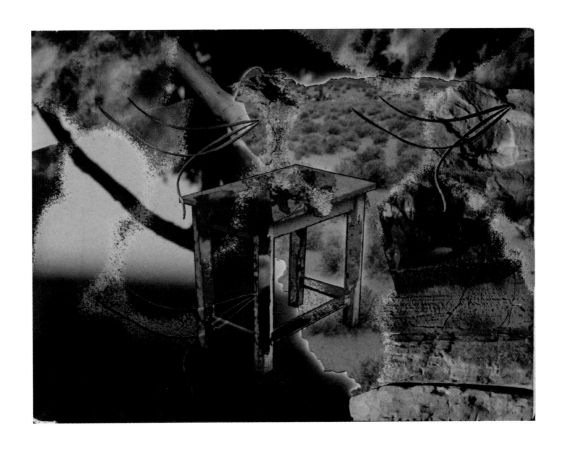

Dixie's Table, 1983

Remote Control, 1990

Pupal Bingo, 2003

Trouble in the Image, 1996

64

PERMANENT TRANSIT: THE FILMS OF PAT O'NEILL
BY PAUL ARTHUR

I had to admit to myself that I lived for nights like these, moving across the city's great broken body, making connections among its millions of cells. I had a crazy wish that some day before I died, if I made all the right neural connections, the city would come all the way alive, like the Bride of Frankenstein.
—Ross Macdonald, *The Instant Enemy*

For the inaugural issue of the journal *Dreamworks*, Pat O'Neill filed a "Dream Report," dated 1977, that sounds remarkably close to a passage from one of his films. Indeed, like the elegantly uncanny moving pictures that anchor his career, O'Neill's sampling of unconscious scenography operates in the gap between the hermetic and demotic, between image-fragments whose significance remains obscure and iconography familiar enough be lodged in our cultural memory banks. He describes a room with peeling walls, broken windows opening onto a view of pristine sky. There is a "desert spa built out of volcanic rock" in the distance, with a vintage Oldsmobile perched on the driveway. Removing a hubcap from the automobile, the dreamer discovers a secret cache of still photos. While examining a shot of a calendar pinup girl, the light begins to fade.[1] As is true of O'Neill's films, a sense of place and of architectural detail take precedence over human figures and their activities. Transiency, ostensibly the default position for all dream experience, informs even static views of quotidian objects. It is possible to read the decaying room as a *camera obscura*, for O'Neill a primal and recurrent site of fast-motion processions of light. Defying physical laws of gravity and mass, a landscape may be shown as nested with frames sporting divergent spatial configurations. Car, rock, photo—they are elements of a familiar dance in which machines couple with natural elements in spasms of categorical inversion. The almost irresistible temptation is to turn O'Neill's report into a kind of rebus, which if carefully deciphered might illuminate his otherwise obscure principles of cinematic construction. From the sleep of unreason, an idiolect emerges.

Yet the trouble with this line of inquiry is obvious. Without recourse to the language of psychoanalysis—by which visual symbols are reread as symptoms—the superficial linkage of dream account and movie images results in merely reinforcing, not decoding, visual patterns observable in the films themselves. Moreover, the particular fabric of O'Neill's work, especially its distance from canonical forms of expressive subjectivity, rebuffs the standard tools of psychoanalytic interpretation. To be sure, several less quixotic insights can be culled from the journal entry: that autobiographically-inflected dream material constitutes a surprising source for the filmmaker's creative imagination; further, that his fascination with subconscious imagery taps into a legacy of Surrealism in art and film. Neither idea has been closely pursued in critical writings or in interviews, and neither will receive adequate treatment here. It is worth noting, however, that the desire to incorporate or imitate the condensatory power of dreams had been a key project in earlier avant-garde film styles, a project that gradually fell into disfavor at about

the time O'Neill began to make films.[2] While it would be unproductive to approach O'Neill's work as, say, a late species of the Trance Film or experimental psychodrama, addressing it through modernist paradigms of material self-reference or ironic treatment of pop culture—heretofore the dominant approach—proves to be equally shortsighted. The point is that among the challenges, and substantial rewards, arising from the filmmaker's forty-year trail of movie alchemy is difficulty in finding a consistent angle of vision, a stable historical or morphological niche, from which to address its inclusive achievement. That this is so despite ample evidence of recurrent visual patterns and enduring philosophical concerns is, paradoxically, part and parcel of the oeuvre's larger significance. In this sense the films are at once attuned to, and examples of, deeply liminal objects—interstitial and in constant flux even within the arena of critical discourse.

A measure of their slippery status is glimpsed in responses that have little or nothing to do with issues of personal or social meaning, cultural allusion, iconographic or formal inheritance. Instead, the patent complexity and elusiveness of O'Neill's images tend to elicit agonizingly detailed descriptions of what happens on screen at any given moment; how an image first appears then is transformed, rather than what it contributes to our understanding of the world. Although analogies are offered to the experience of perceptual testing or "puzzle-solving," the tone of such reports suggests a bout of *ambient* dreaming. It is as if the need to ratify in memory the dazzling surface of screen activity privileges one's immediate, sensual impressions at the expense of broader motifs, themes, tropes. A typical conclusion holds that O'Neill's films "pose to the viewer the general problem of finding a way through a discontinuous multiplicity of meaning."[3] When not making a case for irreducible ambiguity or diffuseness in confrontation with the work, commentators have resorted to oddly misleading parallels: psychedelic tripping, TV channel-surfing, "dynamic graffiti."[4] O'Neill himself has not exactly discouraged assessments grounded in indeterminacy. In program notes for *Saugus Series*, he writes that separate scenes in the film connect to form small stories, "recapitulations of remembered events and feelings told somehow from the vantage point of one who is half awake, on the magic edge of entering or leaving consciousness."[5] He has, conversely, repeatedly called attention to affinities with factual cinemas, from archival history compilations to science lectures and industrial training shorts: "I conceive of films that are very close to documentaries, but they're not."[6] The straddling of generic options does not stop there: as early as 1976, O'Neill considered experimenting with

1. Pat O'Neill, "Dream Report," *Dreamworks* 1, no.1 (Spring 1980): 32–33.
2. For an analysis of the role of dream imagery in the early American avant-garde, see P. Adams Sitney, *Visionary Film: The American Avant-Garde, 1943–2000*, 3rd ed. (New York: Oxford University Press, 2002), 3–15.

3. Grahame Weinbren and Christine Noll Brinckmann, "Selective Transparencies: Pat O'Neill's Recent Films," *Millennium Film Journal*, no. 6 (Spring 1980): 53.
4. See Mitch Tuchman, "Pat O'Neill: In All Directions," *Film Comment* (July–August 1976): 24, 26; and Tricia Crane, "Los Locals: Pat O'Neill," *L.A. Style* 6, no.6 (November 1990): 36, respectively.

methods of commercial storytelling: "One of the ideas was that I would begin to work with dialogue, begin to work with actors... knowing exactly how to finally get the lines down, get the story down."[7] This impulse would finally reach fruition twenty years later. The common belief that procedures associated with Hollywood narrative, with documentary, and with the avant-garde are mutually incompatible is untenable, a gross canard perpetrated by a combination of marketing demands and film-historical blindness. Nonetheless, mapping the terrain of a film career for which established generic, technical, and stylistic boundaries are merely provisional—if not altogether illusory, like a desert mirage—requires at the least a point of departure and a willingness to court disorientation. In addition, it is helpful to bear in mind a mythic ground zero, whose coordinates dictate institutional as well as social possibilities. For lack of a better moniker, we will call this central region "Los Angeles."

ITINERARIES

Among supporters of the movement, the public anonymity of avant-garde filmmakers is a longstanding joke. An ironic acknowledgment of that anonymity can be gleaned from O'Neill's stealthy appearances in his films, something like a disenfranchised version of Alfred Hitchcock's famous cameos. In *The Decay of Fiction*, he takes a brief turn as a hard-boiled pulp writer, or perhaps gossip columnist, hunkered over an ancient typewriter. The opening tableau in *Foregrounds* casts him as an inert figment of nature, a recessive backyard monument. In *Trouble in the Image*, he pops onto the screen to scribble a glowing figure with a long stick, the incarnation of a cinematic sorcerer (or just an apprentice). *Water and Power* finds him, among other poses, with a bag on his head. Verbal references and iconographic "stand-ins" widen the metaphoric scope of role-playing to include an action painter, jazzman, detective, naturalist, and sandwich maker. Hence it is more than a cliche to suggest that O'Neill has worn a multitude of cinematic hats, several of which have received quite literal representation, like the floating porkpie at the end of *Saugus Series*. Mitch Tuchman once characterized his aesthetic presence as an amalgam of tinker, prospector, and magician. Born a century earlier, O'Neill might well have assisted the invention of the automobile, a prominent object among a cluster of surrogate movie-machines crisscrossing the body of his work. For all their gleaming wizardry, however, the films retain vestiges of a handmade, Rube Goldberg funkiness—the machine as unreliable contraption. Nor can we ignore avatars from the animal kingdom: dogs, snakes, and bugs are recurrent motifs, but the pack rat and chameleon are both appropriate, if unspoken, totems.

Looking beyond the screen, O'Neill's personal trajectory is only slightly less steeped in allegory. While studying art and industrial design at UCLA, he began a transition into independent filmmaking that is itself emblematic of the period. Unwilling to abandon sculpture or still photography, he enacted a pivotal tenet of the nascent counterculture in which restrictive divisions among creative disciplines—indeed, among cultural initiatives in general—would be jettisoned in favor of more "organic," almost invariably multi-media, approaches. In O'Neill's case, the idea of cinema as meta-practice surfaces, for example, in his association with the light show collective Single Wing Turquoise Bird and his early interest in gallery installations employing film loops, a means of extending or supplementing more linear exercises in moving light phenomena. Joining the experimental movement during an era of notable expansion, O'Neill contributed to efforts aimed at gaining greater public visibility for avant-garde film, mainly

5. "Some Notes by the Filmmaker," a handout at the Millennium Film Workshop screening, November 2, 1974, n.p.
6. Quoted in Tuchman, "Pat O'Neill," 26.
7. Ibid., 28.

8. David E. James provides a synoptic discussion of the history of alternative film institutions in L.A. in "Toward a Geo-Cinematic Hermeneutics: Representations of Los Angeles in Non-Industrial Cinema—*Killer of Sheep* and *Water and Power*," *Wide Angle* 20, no.3 (July 1998): 29–33. See also: Samir Hachem, "Now You See Them, Now You Don't: Exhibition and Distribution of Avant-Garde Film in L.A.," *Journal: Southern California Art*

through participation in the "Genesis" project, two traveling programs of shorts that achieved unprecedented commercial distribution in the late sixties. Such attempts at developing new venues or formal templates for the display of unorthodox images foreshadow recent excursions into 35mm production and interactive DVD-ROM. For a filmmaker whose primal unit of articulation is the self-limiting frame rather than the sequence or cut, his career exudes a quality of unslaked restlessness underwritten by a dread of confinement. That this dynamic reflects in part the plight of someone whose life and work have been moored to a single, notoriously contradictory geographic setting is a topic to which we will return.

A dozen years removed from UCLA, O'Neill was leaving an imprint on practically every facet of the local film scene. He was a founding member of Oasis, a collective devoted to the exhibition and discussion of alternative cinema, one of only two such organizations in the area.[8] His influence as formal and informal mentor, as well as frequent technical collaborator, acquired legendary status. A founding faculty member of the film and video program at California Institute of the Arts (CalArts), he tutored a younger generation of media artists for whom he functioned as a bridge between older avant-garde styles and fresh perspectives that cast aside entrenched oppositions of film versus video, narrative versus abstraction, self-expression versus technical polish. Frustrated by what he refers to as the "stop-start" rhythm of academic life, in 1976 O'Neill parlayed a growing proficiency at optical printing into a freelance special-effects business, setting up a small studio that hired and trained a number of younger makers. By the 1980s, this cadre was reviving the energies of a regional avant-garde that had ebbed and flowed since the late forties. As usual, Pat O'Neill generated a soft-spoken clout at the hub of disparate activities.

Although the postwar avant-garde can trace its semi-official inauguration to Los Angeles—courtesy of Maya Deren, Kenneth Anger, and Curtis Harrington—the sorts of centralized bohemian enclaves and institutional support structures that spurred the growth of alternative filmmaking in, say, New York and San Francisco failed to materialize in Southern California. To the extent that L.A. was later able to claim a distinct identity within the movement, it revolved around faintly derogatory notions of technical fluency, what by 1971 David Curtis had labeled "optical/kinetic" performance, a rough equivalent to the artworld epithet "finish fetish."[9] As exemplary instances of this tendency, O'Neill's films—at least prior to the release of *Water and Power*—had to contend with critical appraisals by which the formal investi-

gation of filmic "surface" carried negative connotations.[10] In the following discussions, I use the term as shorthand for a variety of discursive features with social and ecological as well as aesthetic implications.

A brief detour around the arcana of movie technology is necessary at the outset. The multi-planar composite image, as facilitated by the optical printer, looms over O'Neill's work in a manner similar to the way camera movement undergirds the films of Michael Snow or the splice functions as epistemological nexus in the first stages of Stan Brakhage's massive oeuvre. It should be clear that their films are in no sense *about* their signature technical operations; rather, for each artist a specific aspect of the production process served to epitomize creative exigencies of individual skill, materiality, and aesthetic vision. In this light O'Neill's printer is at once a dream space and science laboratory geared to the mutation of extant images. The range of printing options recruited by O'Neill include stationary and traveling mattes, bi-packing, color modulation, looping, image enlargement and reduction, even subtitling. To compose with a printer is essentially to render images of images, a setup that retreats in precise increments from the photographing of external reality. Often considered a streamlined or semi-automated task, printing for O'Neill can be as spontaneous as diary recording and as labor intensive as cell animation. Since the material circumstances of projection and rephotography are intrinsic to the regimen of optical printing, it is not surprising that the films are studded with visual tropes referencing one or the other state—internal screens or vignettes are prodigious. The reflexive effect here is not simply to call attention to cinematic ontology, to strip the seductive veneer off movie illusions, but to immerse the viewer in a sinuous reciprocity of man-made and natural shapes, processes and environments. Nor is the rhetorical fallout derived from melding contrary elements uniform in mood or in social critique. Nothing stands still in this work even if the impetus to motion is understood as a force imposed from outside—at its most basic, the luxurious, inexorable progress of a filmstrip through the apparatus.

Magazine 29 (Summer 1981): 59–64.

9. David Curtis, *Experimental Cinema: A Fifty-Year Evolution* (New York: Dell Publishing, 1971), 164.

10. Grahame Weinbren and Christine Noll Brinckmann argue that a concern for "surface" effects in O'Neill is critically obtuse; hopefully, I bypass this charge by elevating the idea

of surface into something like a metacritical discourse: "The O'Neill Landscape: Four Scenes from *Foregrounds*," *Millennium Film Journal*, nos. 4/5 (Summer/Fall 1979): 103.

EXQUISITE CORPSES, MECHANICAL BRIDES

The titling of O'Neill's early work is instructive. Of nine films completed by 1976, four reference or allude to specific places while three evoke mechanical processes. His first film, *By the Sea*, made in collaboration with Robert Abel, gravitates to a site that in various guises—found footage, superimposition, optical deformation—constitutes one vector in a triad of richly symbolic settings, in this case the western edge where water meets land. *Saugus Series*, indicating a town in an outlying Los Angeles valley, summons a second crucial landscape encompassing the tableaux of brushy foothills and desert. The final location, discernible in the title *Bump City*, draws on commercial-residential zones etched by the region's intricate urban-suburban design. Pertinent to his entire body of work, including recent features, the notion of "setting" does not assume a stable or even foundational space upon which human, animal, or celestial activities are mapped cinematically. Instead, topographic features are subjected to chains of transformation, leaving them not illegible but certainly penetrated and/or surrounded by alien phantasms. O'Neill, always a keen observer of his hometown, has consistently presented locations associated with leisure activities and tourism; in fact, it would not be far-fetched to imagine the films as warped travelogues or, more suggestively, oneiric tour guides.

David E. James, addressing the local topography in relation to O'Neill's films, invokes Michel Foucault's idea of "heterotopia," the coexistence of several otherwise incompatible spaces within a single real location.[11] Rayner Banham's well-known thesis that L.A. is comprised of four separate ecologies—beaches, foothills, central flatlands, and freeways—offers another model relevant to the filmmaker's segmented, visually layered treatment of place.[12] Among the idiosyncratic trademarks of O'Neill landscapes is their imbrication with technology, specifically with manual tools and the remnants of nineteenth-century steel-and-steam mechanics. Absent from this vision, however, is any hint of Romantic ideology, of nostalgic longing for the unspoiled pastoral amidst the wreckage of industrial society. For starters, even the most isolated locations have long since been colonized by representational technologies of still photography and movies. In addition, the recording of certain industrial products possesses for O'Neill a fascination and formal beauty no less compelling than that of a waterfall or red rock butte. Machines regularly appear as weird species of mutated flora; conversely, natural elements take on the attributes of internal combustion engines. In one vista, a hand trowel sticks up from the horizon like a national monument; in another, Old Faithful spits and wheezes in fast motion like a

creaky air compressor; if the moon is tweaked to chug across the sky like a freight train, tiny paper projection screens on the desert floor are made to behave like tumbleweed.

As was readily apparent to commentators a century ago, the movie experience provides an animated window onto exotic locales whose manifestation is governed by a series of mechanical operations. If O'Neill's work, especially his later films, echoes with any yearning for the past, it is for a blue collar world of manual praxis, a realm inhabited not only by crankshafts and acetylene torches but by the optical printer, now a photochemical dinosaur in an age of digital CGI.[13] It is in this register that the title *Runs Good* recalls ads for used automobiles—as O'Neill suggests—as well as the comforting chatter of movie equipment. *Easyout* is the name of a compound for loosening rusted engine bolts, *7362* the number of a Kodak print stock. The relationship between landscape and technology, as mediated by human or social desiderata, is a venerable theme in American literature and art. Leaving aside O'Neill's highly personalized method of image construction, his version of this quandary is unusual on several counts: the opposed terms are never universalized, they are temporal and site-specific; technophobic impulses are rare despite overt and covert generic allegiances to science-fiction; the expression of anarchic breakdown as an alternative to repressive regimentation lacks patently liberatory or utopian connotations.

By the Sea opens a major thematic seam involving the mechanization of human movement. The first section lays out quick, close shots in black and white of denizens of Muscle Beach in Santa Monica—mostly men, with a few women—exercising on outdoor gymnastic equipment, flexing and stretching in front of sedentary visitors. Then a chunk of the same shots gets repeated in new rhythms, this time printed in high-contrast, a process that collapses the impression of depth and turns comely bodies in motion into grotesque, inky cartoon figures. The film has the feel of a simple demonstration: "see how strange these preening paragons can look when their images are zapped through rephotography?" Nonetheless, two important axioms refined in subsequent films make their initial appearance. First, the lines separating normal human locomotion, biomorphic movement, and abstraction are unstable at best. Second, the explicit segmentation of filmic structure almost inevitably raises larger, not exclusively formal issues of continuity, repetition, and cyclicality; these syntactical features, moreover, can be summarized by the broad notion of "looping" as endemic of the moviemaking process.

11. James, "Toward a Geo-Cinematic Hermeneutics," 26.
12. See Rayner Banham, *Los Angeles: The Architecture of Four Ecologies* (New York: Penguin, 1971).
13. In James's related formulation, the display of technology in *Water and Power* "bespeaks a longing for a world of mechanical reproduction... a nostalgia for visual precision, for full visual sensuousness, for vision itself." "Toward a Geo-Cinematic Hermeneutics," 49.

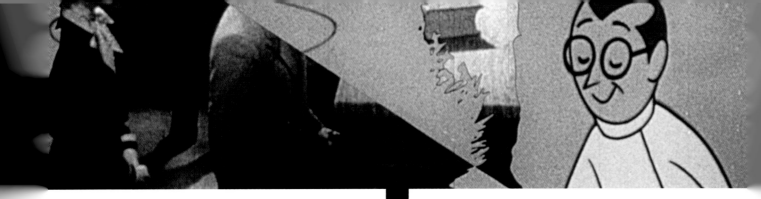

By the Sea, in its deflation of the body beautiful, sustains parodic reference to the second half of Leni Riefenstahl's 1938 *Olympia*. Although linked by reputation to the psychedelic "head trip," *7362* revisits one of the cornerstones of the European avant-garde of the twenties, Fernand Léger and Dudley Murphy's 1924 *Ballet mecanique*. O'Neill's initial plunge into split-screen aesthetics, the film reanimates shots of an oil pump and a female dancer, printing mirrored variations of their movements split along a vertical axis. Besides being edited into aggressively strobelike patterns, the original images have been further denatured by intense color permutations—especially in the red-purple-blue range—and the flipping of foreground shapes from positive to negative. The result has predictably garnered comparisons to a high-speed Rorschach test, flashing abstract patterns onto which an individual subjectivity projects anxieties or desires. A stronger implication lies in O'Neill's erotic coupling of female body and mechanical rig. In Léger and Murphy's film, isolated fragments of a woman's lips, eyes, and other body parts are juxtaposed with the movements of factory components and common utensils in order to secure their metaphoric identity: bodies are like machines and machines possess similar aesthetic properties to the human form. In *7362*, the presence of machines requires no backhanded defense while the yin/yang prospect of categorical merging remains exempt from either horror or celebration.

The human-machine interface is a staple of Hollywood sci-fi. Among canonical directors, Stanley Kubrick mined this theme in a comically corrosive vein in *Dr. Strangelove*; shortly after the completion of *7362*, Kubrick then capped his ruminations in another numerical title, *2001* (a film on which West Coast avant-gardist Jordan Belson provided uncredited technical assistance). *Runs Good* unveils a malignant, seemingly post-apocalyptic future in which "natural" prerogatives of human, animal, and mechanical life forms have been thoroughly confounded. As is true of sci-fi in general, envisioning the future is coextensive with dissecting the present. The shadow of Vietnam and a revulsion towards the triumph of American consumerism—what Guy Debord had dubbed "The Society of the Spectacle"—fuel an overall tone that uncharacteristically verges on anger. Engaging in the sort of sour fetishism that seeps from Bruce Conner's collage films, *Runs Good* is constructed on a similar platform of quirky found footage, mostly bargain basement newsreels, educational science tracts, and Hollywood B-movies. A stentorian voice informs us that: "In the great cities, the legendary worship of the snake has degenerated into sideshows." Alarmingly, a repressive sideshow mentality has run amok, evident in not just in parades and magic tricks but in shots of wartime combat, a football game, TV ads, a wedding, domestic routines. From scenes at a dog show we gather that mankind has tamed, caged, and reprogrammed every animal instinct; on the other hand, a woman crawls on all-fours like a dog in an antique porn clip while another performs a looped, mechanized striptease timed to the countdown of a digital clock.

The soundtrack, by Cisko Curtis, is packed with electronic burbles, melodramatic mood music from the Forties and Fifties, and bizarre statements lifted from documentary narrations. Over time, O'Neill's audio collaborations expand dramatically in technical and semantic sophistication, yet they have continued to reflect the same collage ethos underlying *Runs Good*. Like *7362*, the film follows a loosely additive trajectory in which an image skein builds in complex interaction with sound—cued by the onset of techniques such as traveling mattes, alterations in speed or hue, superimposition—then reaches a point of intensification before tailing off. Unlike his first two films, discrete sections are not cordoned off by fades or, as in *Saugus Series*, by numbered episodes. Mitch Tuchman draws a helpful analogy between hybridized, multi-planar compositions in *Runs Good* and paintings by Larry Rivers, in particular the acclaimed "Washington Crossing the Delaware."[14] In passing, it is worth noting that there exists a wealth of iconographic and formal congruities between O'Neill and a contemporaneous cadre of American painters including Robert Rauschenberg, Jasper Johns, James Rosenquist and, from a less mainstream perspective, Jess, for whom layered, heterogeneous image-fields ripened into an emblem of late-sixties culture.

Easyout and *Down Wind* are slightly less hectic, or agitated, in design. Both percolate with moments of abstract animation and occasional strobe effects but also seem to contain more original footage and passages less prone to optical distortion. Junctures between shots are somewhat clearer and despite what was evolving into a marked preference for fast-motion and time-lapse recording, there are moments that tease odd juxtapositions in content or scale from relatively straightforward camera views. In one enticing shot from *Down Wind*, saggy male bathers wade in a shallow pond while in the extreme foreground an ominously large swan tends to its feathers. At first glance it strikes us that this conjunction must be the product of technical sleight-of-hand but that impression is vacated almost immediately. Awareness of the flow of time, and with it a sense of anticipation or memory, allows for a change of pace with imagery so concentrated it gives the impression of unfolding in a single prolonged instant, the lyrical avant-garde's eternal present.

14. Tuchman, "Pat O'Neill," 26.

Civilization and its discontents, as expressed through representations of anthropology's raw and cooked behavior, is a subtext in both films. Shots of wild animals mating collide with scenes featuring domesticated rituals.

Easyout pays homage to yet another avant-garde classic, Buñuel and Dalí's *Un Chien andalou* (1928), by way of humorous subversions of bourgeois settings and allusions to obsessional images, such as O'Neill's superimposition of giant ants overrunning a humdrum suburban intersection. For good measure, he tosses in some nonsensical Surrealist subtitles: "Meanwhile," "Several days later"—talisman displayed to ward off linear narrative, the vehicle of middle-class spectacle. Perhaps a deeper bond to Surrealist aims is manifest in O'Neill's accretion of disjunct sequences, a process with parallels to the fabled "Exquisite Corpse." Extending the intellectual parlor game, in which a figure drawing is produced by successive artists without knowledge of what was previously drawn, Dalí and Buñuel relied on "psychic automatism" for the scripting of *Un Chien andalou:* "When an image or idea appeared the collaborators discarded it immediately if it was derived from remembrance, or from their cultural pattern or if, simply, it had a conscious association with an earlier idea."[15] The image flow in *Easyout*, as in most of O'Neill's work, suggests a series of mini-movies grafted onto a tenuous thematic skeleton, a sort of animated, one-man Exquisite Corpse.

Down Wind, freighted as it is with unprepossessing vacation footage, is largely devoid of the crowds that populate earlier films, signaling a renewed engagement with the spatial paradoxes and asymmetries of non-urban settings. Here as elsewhere, aqueous and barren landscapes are what remain when the thrum of human presence subsides. Frequent traveling shots, taken from car windows, are a perfect emblem of O'Neill's transient screen doings. Deftly tapping into nonfiction codes evocative of the travelogue and home movie, *Down Wind* nudges intertextual affiliations toward far-flung, ostensibly antagonist, arenas. It is said that his films are unique in their idiosyncrataic application of recondite movie technology; nonetheless, it is impossible to relegate them to a "rustic" sphere of unbridled, detached subjectivity. Nothing cinematic is foreign to O'Neill. Eluding the snares of formalist reduction yet not satisfactorily housed under a *postmodern* rubric of ironic pastiche, his output circumvents polarities of hermetic indifference and transparent polemic.

Last of the Persimmons, by any criterion a minor undertaking, is still a witty reminder of the filmmaker's inveterate contrariness with regard to dominant media. It resembles, on the one hand, a frothy, six-minute newsreel segment on the growth cycle and eating pleasures of an inconspicuous local fruit, a hermeneutic ditty invaded by stray, if hardly random, fragments of cartoons and animated drawings and buoyed by a pop song from T-Rex. On the other hand, it could be taken as a sly dig at the cascade of so-called Structural films making the rounds of avant-garde venues in the early seventies. The crux of the Structural method, akin to Minimalism in painting and sculpture, lies is its brandishing of a predetermined overall shape, the rational organization of which is intended to suppress subjectively-motivated image connections.[16] O'Neill has acknowledged the influence of Structural exemplar Michael Snow but was, not surprisingly, a noncombatant in the period's intramural style wars.

Of greater interest is how O'Neill avoided a principal aesthetic dilemma honed by the avant-garde of the seventies and early eighties. Briefly, the most diverse and responsive way of creating meaning in film—not coincidently, also the cheapest—is through the mobilization of editing. The imperative of shot-by-shot collisions, as advocated and practiced by poetic master Stan Brakhage, was sharply contested in the wake of Andy Warhol's flagrant recourse in to unbroken camera takes, or single-shot movies. Structural filmmaking refitted the potential of editing to simple mathematical formulae or logical propositions. By the mid-eighties, a return to narrative was endorsed, in part, as a way out of the poetic/formulaic impasse. By the making of *Saugus Series*, and continuing through *Sidewinder's Delta* and *Foregrounds,* O'Neill had found an alternative route around the issue of sequentiality. In program notes to the former, he explains that, "Each of the parts arose from some idea of discontinuity; each once of them features some confrontation between discontinuous units of space and time—in other words, contradictions."[17] *Saugus Series* is composed of seven, semi-autonomous segments held loosely together by a group of interrelated formal gestures and a cluster of motifs. A few typically oblique allusions, to Van Gogh's work boots and to Max Ernst's hats, do not add up to a disquisition on art history, even though this is arguably O'Neill's most "painterly" work.

To be sure, he has grappled with the conceptual torque exerted by editing: "My interest in relationships between elements in static shots has led me to make films that either have no cuts, or that have pauses between shots."[18] Hence for him a reckoning of sequential meaning may not be "cohesive unless you can see it as a kind of journal, a collection of entries all by the same person but at different times and places."[19] David James has used

15. Bunuel is quoted in Sitney, *Visionary Film*, 4.
16. Once again, the best summary of the Structural film aesthetic is in Sitney, *Visionary Film*, 347–70.
17. "Some Notes by the Fimmmaker," n.p.

18. David E. James, "An Interview with Pat O'Neill," *Millennium Film Journal*, nos. 30/31 (Fall 1997): 121.
19. Ibid., 127.
20. Ibid.

the term "dossier-like compilations" to describe the effect; an equally cogent trope is the filmic sketchbook. According to O'Neill, the source of enunciation for this activity is "an individual who wanders the land and from time to time stops to comment on it."[20] Despite the films' deflection of storytelling baggage, O'Neill's comment suggests a sidelong relation to narrative as the allegorical inscription of places visited, inhabited, "studied," with the proviso that geographic locations are *a priori* overlaid with a backlog of cultural associations. Notwithstanding intermittent references to a claustrophobic, two-dimensional surface of TV shows and televisual "noise," the spatial drift in *Saugus Series* is toward open landscapes.

Sidewinder's Delta was initially imagined as a kind of indirect Western, a meditation on the myth of wilderness. The title conjures a riverbed full of snakes—creatures that move by thrusting their bodies forward in a series of loops, recalling the mechanical gist of optical printer and film projector—but delta is also the scientific symbol for change. What exactly is being transformed is itself always in flux, always enigmatic: it might be a set of crusty pictorial codes, a perceptual reflex, or the conditions of genre. In several films, a reflexive agent of change is represented by giant hands posed in the middle of rural perspectives. Two pivotal locations, the artist's studio and the desert, define the limits of O'Neill's visual universe. As the films become increasingly ambitious, a sense of balance between these focal points evaporates.

In somewhat broader terms, a spectral itinerary moves O'Neill in restless increments away from the city's social force field, a peregrination that eventually doubles back to take refuse in *The Decay of Fiction*'s condensed, history-haunted architecture. The Western, our culture's favorite conduit for stories about men getting lost in and returning from the wilderness, is one of three Hollywood idioms that ripple across the skin of O'Neill's work. Occasionally said to recalibrate the dynamics of the Western, film noir sports a distinctly urban agenda; it was notorious even in its own period for subjectivized treatments of violence and sexual betrayal. Science fiction, especially during its fifties' cycle of mutant bugs, lizards, et al., narrates the traffic between urban and rural settings as mediated by—generally malign—consequences of uncontrolled technology. At the risk of oversimplifying the generic undertow in what is surely a multifaceted, irregular arc of production, O'Neill's early films display the strongest affinities for sci-fi, the next group leans toward the Western, while his latest projects explore formal and cultural resonances attached to film noir.

IN THE BELLY OF THE BASIN

On a first viewing, the scale and polymorphic mass of *Water and Power* is likely to register as a summation—even a valediction—instead of just another fork in the road. It opens with a high-wire act, a defiance of natural law by human, or technology-assisted, daring. Then as in all new beginnings, there is a fall. A time-lapse low-angle panorama shows a trestle soaring over minuscule beach strollers. As dusk races in, a lone figure appears on the bridge, climbs the railing and plunges into thin air like a shooting star. This setup will reverberate through later sections of the film, the bridge giving way to a pipeline—*the* pipeline, bringing water to Los Angeles—and other metaphors of traversal just as the self-annihilating figure gets resurrected in a spate of disparate roles. Above all, O'Neill's inaugural plunge into the hybridized waters of quasi-feature production—itself a format bridging two traditionally antithetical movie realms—unfolds as a cycle of visual ebbs and flows, accretions and declensions rehearsed as endemic to the region's historical landscape. It is a location portrayed as echoing with corporeal, biological rhythms, a projected body as it were, rife with illusion. And outright deception.[21]

Among filmic discourses to which it pays explicit or indirect tribute, the City Symphony documentaries of the 1920s, including Dziga Vertov's *Man With a Movie Camera* and Walter Ruttman's *Berlin: Symphony of a Great City*, undergird O'Neill's vision insofar as they celebrate the urban matrix as gigantic machine. Predictably, images of mechanized movement work in reciprocity with modernist demands of cinema; it takes an industrial apparatus to capture an industrialized social space. Like Vertov, O'Neill adumbrates the nexus of city life and camera apparatus as a spectrum of functions ranging from image production to image consumption. Unlike Vertov, for whom the "film factory" was an apt model for the organization of society in general, O'Neill's take on Los Angeles's mimetic "dream factory" is tinged with regret, resentment, and ridicule as well as secretive pleasure. That his film is as technically polished as the TV ads and special-effects epics on which it literally depended for sustenance becomes inseparable from the allegory it constructs of a power-laden image unconscious engulfing the L.A. basin. A flickering network of quotations and allusions summons ghosts from Westerns and sci-fi, Cecil B. De Mille spectacles, early Josef von Sternberg dramas, film noir such as *Detour*. Audio composer George Lockwood inserts melodramatic mood music, dialogue clips, and stock sound effects into a nubbly fabric of tabla drumming, electronic noise, and jazz improvisations. Printed titles and voice-over narration unveil tantalizing fragments of more conventional storytelling.[22] These gambits prod the film's meaning in unexpected historical directions, with a

21. For a somewhat jaundiced review of the claims for, and the obstacles faced by, so-called crossover avant-garde features of 1980s, see my "The Last of the Last Machine?," *A Line of Sight: American Avant-Garde Film, 1965 to the Present* (Minneapolis: University of Minnesota Press, forthcoming 2004). In the same volume, I position this film in a slightly different framework from the one I adopt here: "The Western Edge: Oil of L.A. and the Machined Image."

22. O'Neill has published two fragmentary glosses of the script: "*Water and Power*: A Fragmentary Synopsis," *Motion Picture* 3, nos. 1–2 (Winter 1989–90): 19–20; and "*Water and Power*," *Millennium Film Journal*, no. 25 (Summer 1991): 42–49.

given story scrap able to leap unevenly from verbal to visual expression, and vice versa.

At the resplendent core of *Water and Power* is a cluster of time-lapse views recorded with a specially designed, computer-controlled camera program. According to the filmmaker, footage was accumulated slowly, with durations of up to six hours compressed into a matter of seconds. Certain shots required solitary treks into remote regions while others were filmed from downtown buildings. Some scenes appear with scant material alteration; others undergo intensive renovation through mattes and superimpositions, accumulating as many as nine different layers in a single composition. A master trope involving the film image as simultaneous oasis and mirage surfaces frequently in O'Neill's work. Here that idea is decked with unprecedented historical-political significance. There are references not only to tensions between Native American inhabitants and white settlers but to the 1910 laying of the Owens Lake pipeline that spurred the city's remarkable growth. The resulting ecological disaster *cum* miracle, limned in Roman Polansky and Robert Towne's *Chinatown* (1974), is refracted by O'Neill onto the desiderata of motion pictures. In particular, the transformation by the pipeline of a once-fertile valley into a wasteland, and the development of barren terrain into a lush human environment may be read as a process roughly analogous to the way elemental image traits are reordered in O'Neill's films: how what we perceive as hard ground can be rendered as a liquid, how gassy effusions appear to congeal into a solid, and so on.

Within a complex calculus of elemental and man-made properties, O'Neill positions cinema alongside water, heat, and land as aspects of a single ecological system, in which technology is neither inevitably hostile nor naively redemptive. In this fashion fixed formal, symbolic, and topographic oppositions can start to bend and interpenetrate: abstract animation versus straight photography; interior versus exterior; industry versus culture; desert versus city. Once again, the lockstep designs of a mechanized order—seen especially in a series of right-angle time-lapse pans and tilts—are offset by emblems of freewheeling personal creativity, including various musicians and an artist's model posing in a bare studio. Admittedly, figures zip through their routines at super-fast speed yet their presence is never entirely eclipsed by larger, sidereal movements of light. In O'Neill's post-narrative (rather than non-narrative) Los Angeles, history has collapsed, time is definitely out of joint, and we can no longer parse substance from illusion. Regardless, human memory persists and so does the urge to shape an otherwise confusing welter of site-specific impressions.

Although it underwent a long and arduous ontogeny, the release of *Water and Power* at the end of the 1980s marked a culmination of sorts in the avant-garde's pointed revision of film noir codes; examples of this trend include Manuel DeLanda's *Raw Nerves*, Bette Gordon's *Variety*, Yvonne Rainer's *The Man Who Envied Women*, and Lewis Klahr's *In the Month of Crickets*. Of the major Hollywood genres, noir has exerted perhaps the strongest appeal for independent media artists, and it has proved susceptible to radical reinterpretation on at least three counts. First, by critical consensus noir was for its time inordinately drawn to extreme visual stylizations. Second, it spawned Hollywood's most dire, if also conflicted, dramatizations of the plight of America's urban middle class. Finally, noir's thematic blend of paranoia and rebellious sexuality is said to harbor an allegorical connection with the Hollywood studio system's volatile Cold War ambience, and by extension with postwar Los Angeles itself. Mike Davis is one of many cultural commentators to view film noir as the city's populist, perpetual anti-myth.[23]

In the wake of *Water and Power*, O'Neill would extend and refocus, in two sharply contrasting projects, the appropriation of noir as historical cipher for his birthplace. *Trouble in the Image* returns to a segmental, discontinuous method of organization reminiscent of earlier works, and it does so with a vengeance. Subtitled *Works on Film, 1978–1995*, it is possibly O'Neill's most explosive, textually diffuse film, a collection of sketches, tests, outtakes from commercial assignments, and found footage, all of which are optically overhauled and leavened by George Lockwood's intricate soundscape. It begins with an image of swarming birds whose chaotic yet cyclical motion reprises a motif previously associated with moths, abstract dots, and colored lozenges. The heavy, sexualized breathing of an outlaw couple, lifted from the swampy climax of *Gun Crazy*, instills an ominous tone. Scraps of equally portentous voices from the likes of *Kiss Me Deadly* and *Criss Cross* are filtered into subsequent scenes. In typical fashion, O'Neill draws from obscure cowboy movies along with tacky educational science docs, original landscape shots and one riveting time-lapse view of a cavernous Hollywood studio set in the throes of demolition.

Trouble is in several respects distinct from the more capital-intensive films that precede and follow it. Transitions between images have a harder edge, engendered by an unusual number of straight cuts. In addition, a barrage of split-screen compositions employing up to four separate rectangles of extant footage—tinted, solarized, or otherwise denatured—are juxtaposed in rhythmic or thematic patterns. Rotoscoped outlines of human figures or

23. Mike Davis, *City of Quartz* (New York: Vintage, 1990), 21.

animals in motion are superimposed over rigidly divided frames. The effect is less dreamlike or uncanny than that of earlier hybrid images; it is as if the contents of a late-night TV lineup had been bombarded with subatomic particles, splitting them into toxic new arrangements. Spoken fragments from what seem to be commercial movie scripts, in fact written by O'Neill, waft through the sound design creating a verbal parallel for visual locations presented via an unstable array of quick notations. The "trouble" in the title has, predictably, a host of potential meanings: the criminal mayhem distilled from scenes of a TV series; the manner in which images are divided and repeated in aggressive cadences; and the "violence" with which cultural memories are embedded, as well as how they inflect, our waking consciousness.

The Decay of Fiction is as close as O'Neill has come to making scripted, hyper-controlled, feature-length genre narrative. He took his cues from a story type and a model of production redolent of the studio era but nearly extinct in current Hollywood practice, hence the aura of "decay." Paradoxically, the blockbuster paradigm that replaced Hollywood's classical system was fueled by otherworldly stories trafficking in the very sort of special effects over which O'Neill had demonstrated mastery. Fusing setting with subject, *Fiction* hunkers down in L.A.'s defunct Ambassador Hotel, intent on treating the visual exploration of deteriorating rooms and corridors as a lever to pry loose an encrusted double history of actual events and Hollywood fictions, what the filmmaker calls "an intersection of fact and hallucination."[24] Two widely scattered movie traditions inform O'Neill's central location: industry films such as *Grand Hotel* and *The Shining* that cast hotels as emblems of social compartmentalization; and avant-garde works, from Jean Cocteau's *The Blood of a Poet* to Warhol's *The Chelsea Girls*, in which the strange occupants of individual rooms participate in scenarios of forbidden desire.

Fiction opens in a vacant, water-damaged chamber—another version of *camera obscura*—whose billowing drapes convey a spooky agitation. A moment later it becomes clear what, or rather who, is haunting this locale: dialogue from an assortment of film noir; the movement of time etched into walls and passageways; and a coterie of diaphanous black-and-white figures in forties period dress superimposed over full color views of present-day hotel architecture. As it happens, these apparitions are equipped with names, backstories, tangled relationships, even individual nightmares. Their well-worn roles include those of cop, gangster, entertainer, gambler, waitress, maid, floozie. There is a protagonist ("Jack") and a bunch of secondary players deployed in parallel narrative strands. In the course of the film they engage in argument, seduction, betrayal, coercion, and possibly murder. Their dialogues are interwoven with the voices of "real" film noir stalwarts like Robert Mitchum, Joan Crawford, Kirk Douglas, and Dana Andrews.

In conventional Hollywood fare, there is an unmistakable hierarchy of elements that begins with actors' faces and voices and descends in importance through sets and costumes, camerawork, music, and so on. O'Neill has schemed to turn this hierarchy, as it were, inside out. Recall the venerable studio technique of back projection (now obsolete due to the ease of computer imaging) in which a moving exterior backdrop was displayed behind actors performing on a stage. Its purpose was to enhance visual realism yet, frequently, back projection created a phony, eerily disjunct meld of foreground and background space—an imperfect mirage. In *Fiction*, it is the characters that look awkwardly grafted while architectural details have a satisfying, if bedraggled, solidity. To be sure, the semi-transparency of foreground action is a metaphor for how old movies continue to circulate in consciousness; as the filmmaker proclaims, it is the "common condition of stories partly remembered, films partly seen, texts at the margins of memory..."[25] The physical structure in which images are sedimented has, in fact, functioned as a common movie locale, a set used by literally a thousand films and TV shows; it was as well as temporary residence for dozens of celebrities, the home of early Academy Award dinners, and the site of the Robert F. Kennedy assassination.

In O'Neill's *Fiction*, the Ambassador Hotel is, finally, a monument to the city it serviced, indeed to the entire region—an amalgam of Hollywood sound stage, real estate boondoggle, historical catacombs, and amusement park hall of mirrors. Within the context of his wider career, the geometrical spatial coordinates of the Ambassador, its inherent divisions and palpable signs of aging, may be adduced as the flipside, but also the symbol complement, of the desert—a domain of bewildering sightlines, oneiric contrasts, and irregular shapes. In this sense the hotel is the desert's urban double, an oasis for the gathering of mythic as well as social significance. In a phrase coined by Carey McWilliams for his film noir era study of Southern California culture, it is "an island on the land." With benefit of hindsight, it is also the edifice around which O'Neill's films have been moving, in a spasmodic arc of approach and avoidance, from the very beginning.

24. "Film Synopsis," notes distributed for a screening at the New York Film Festival, October 14, 2002, n.p.

25. Ibid.

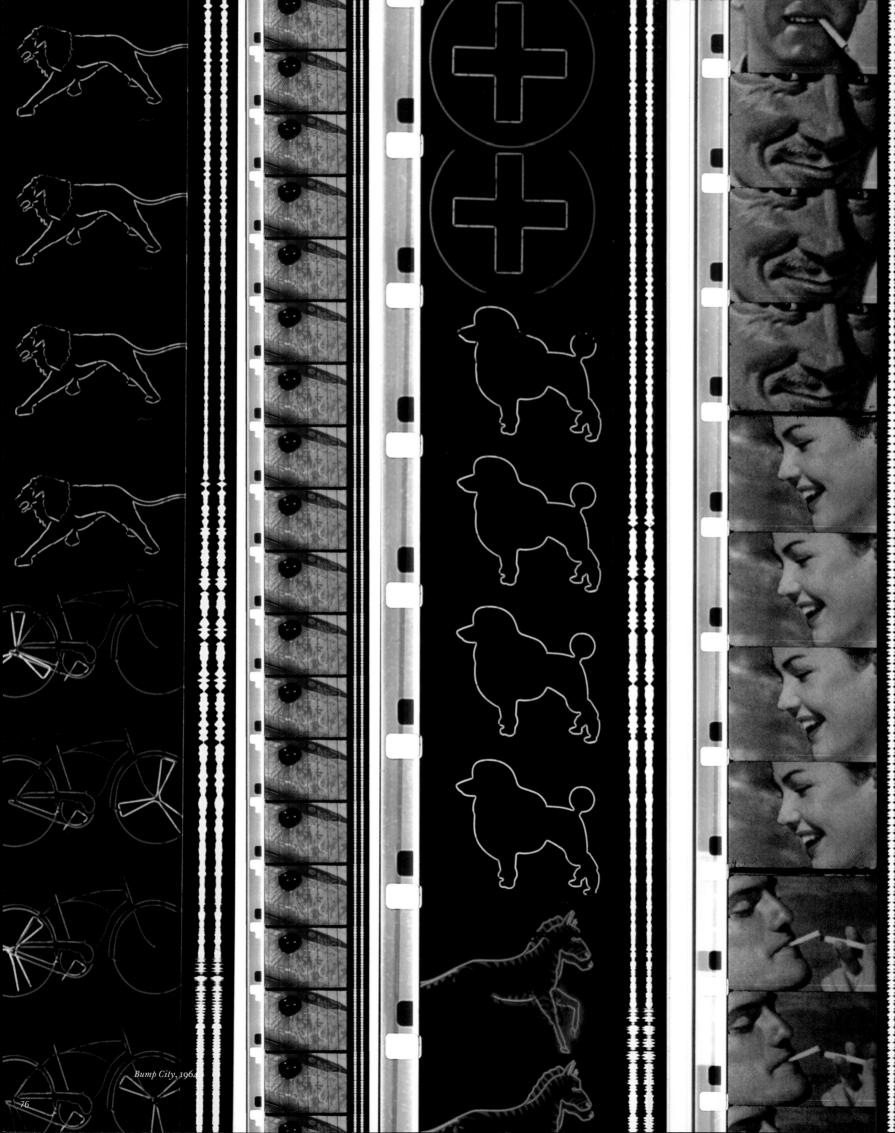

Bump City, 1964

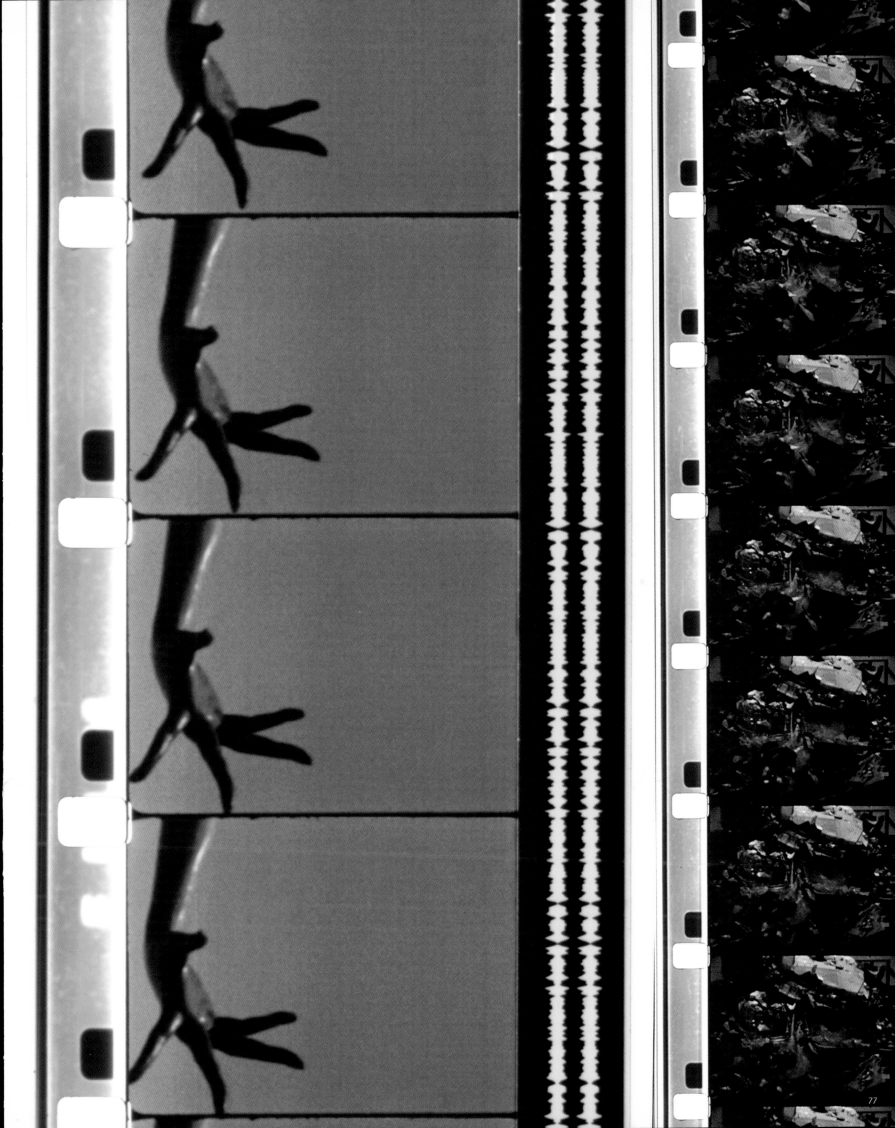

Downdraft, 1998
Collection of Jacqueline Humbert and David Rosenboom, Valencia, California

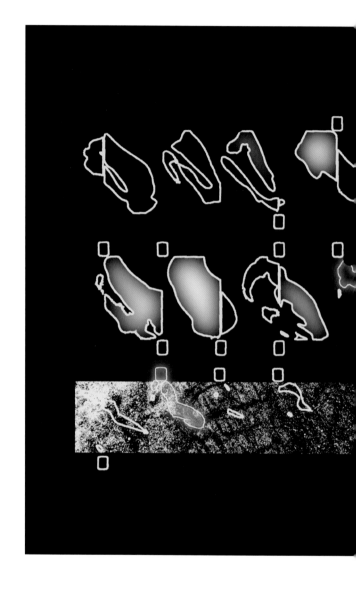

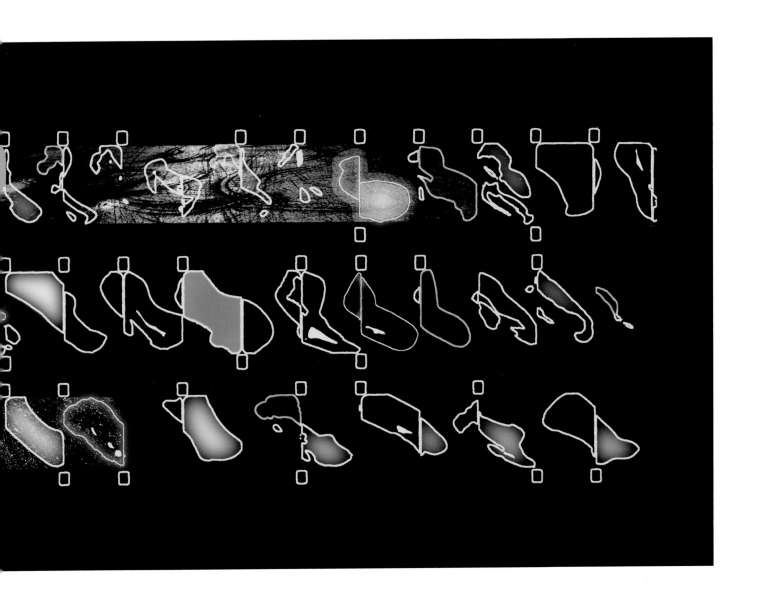

Dance of the Pinheads, 1999

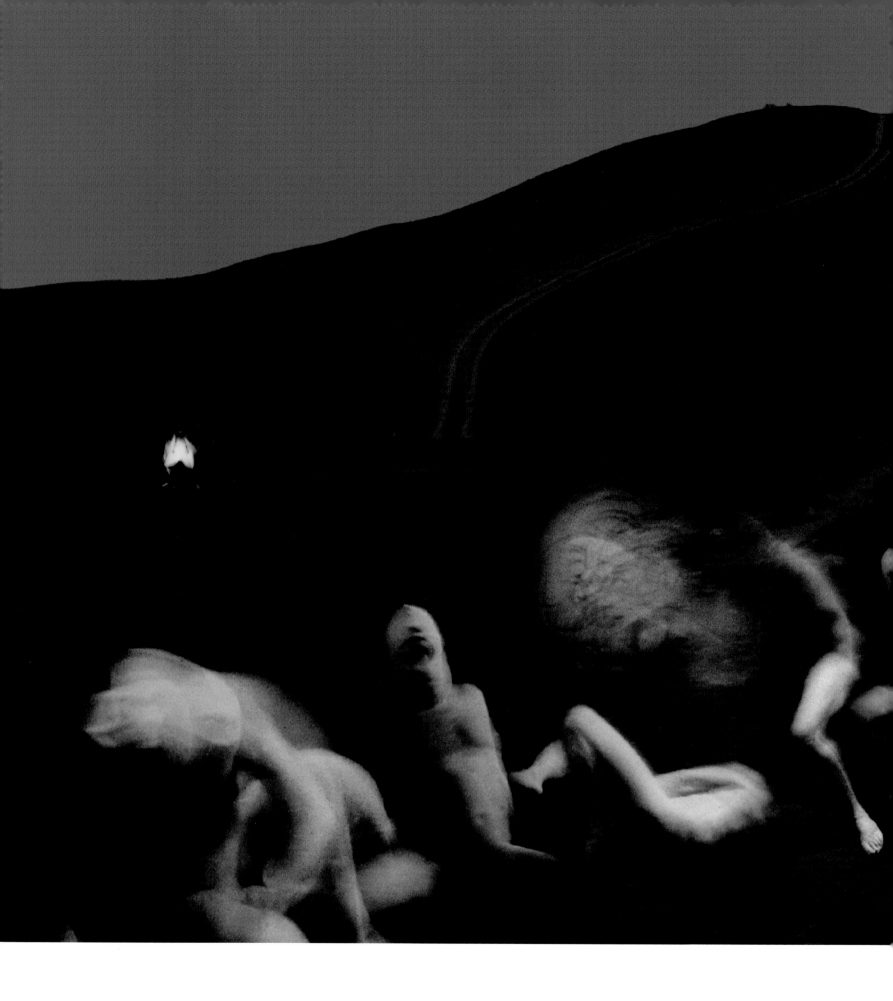

Downhill Bob, 2002

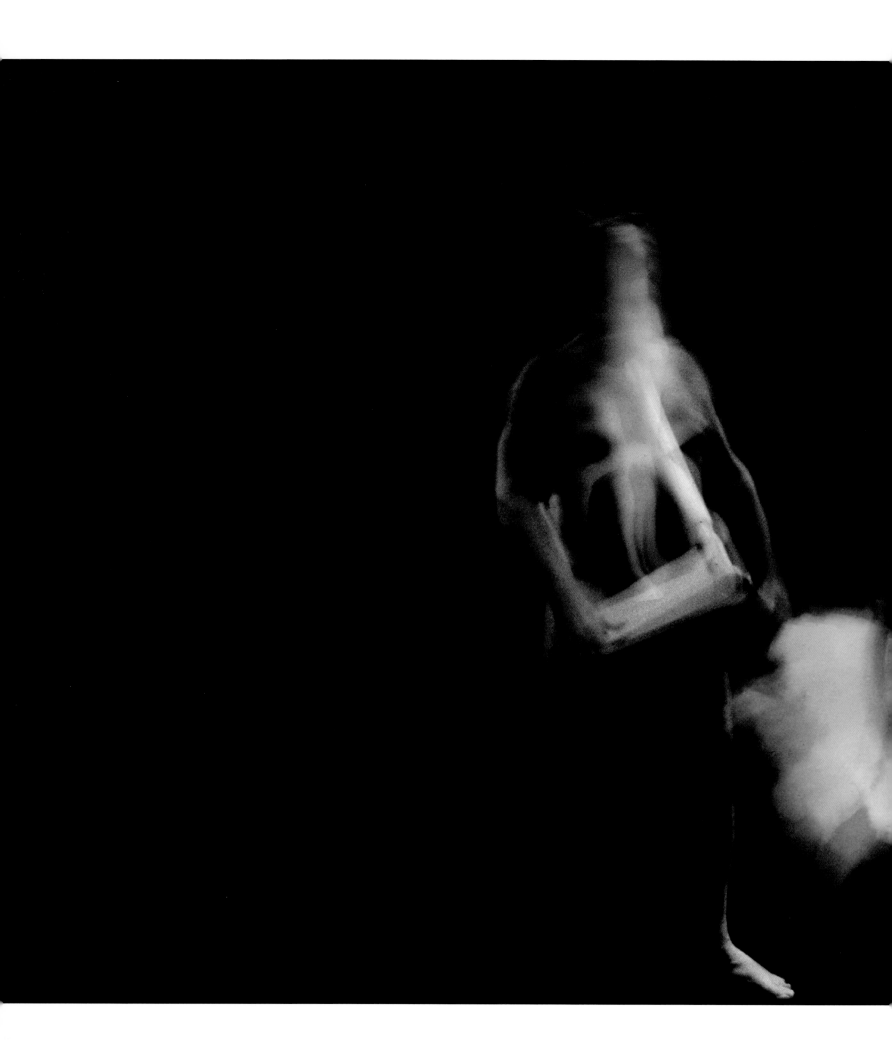

Iceman, 2002

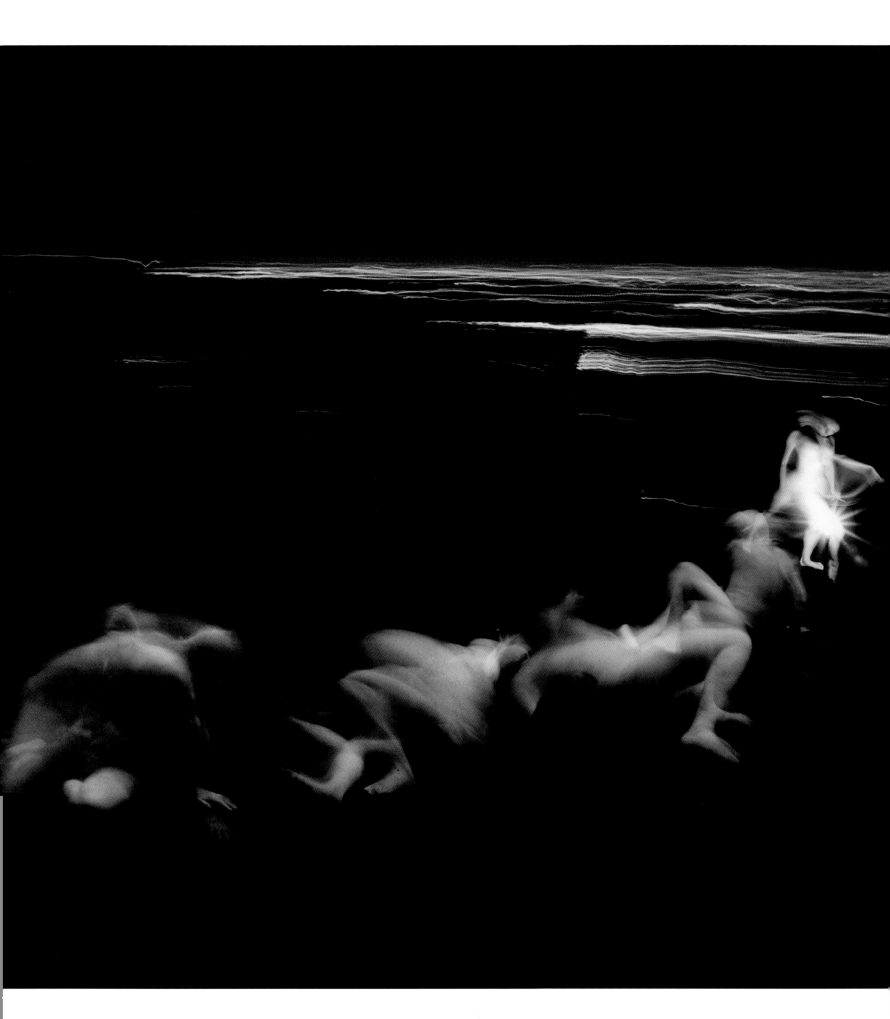

Bastard 1, 2002

Swordfish 1, 2002

Runs Good, 1970

Bascom's Heart, 2003

Y Piso, 2004

SD3, 2003

SD1, 2003

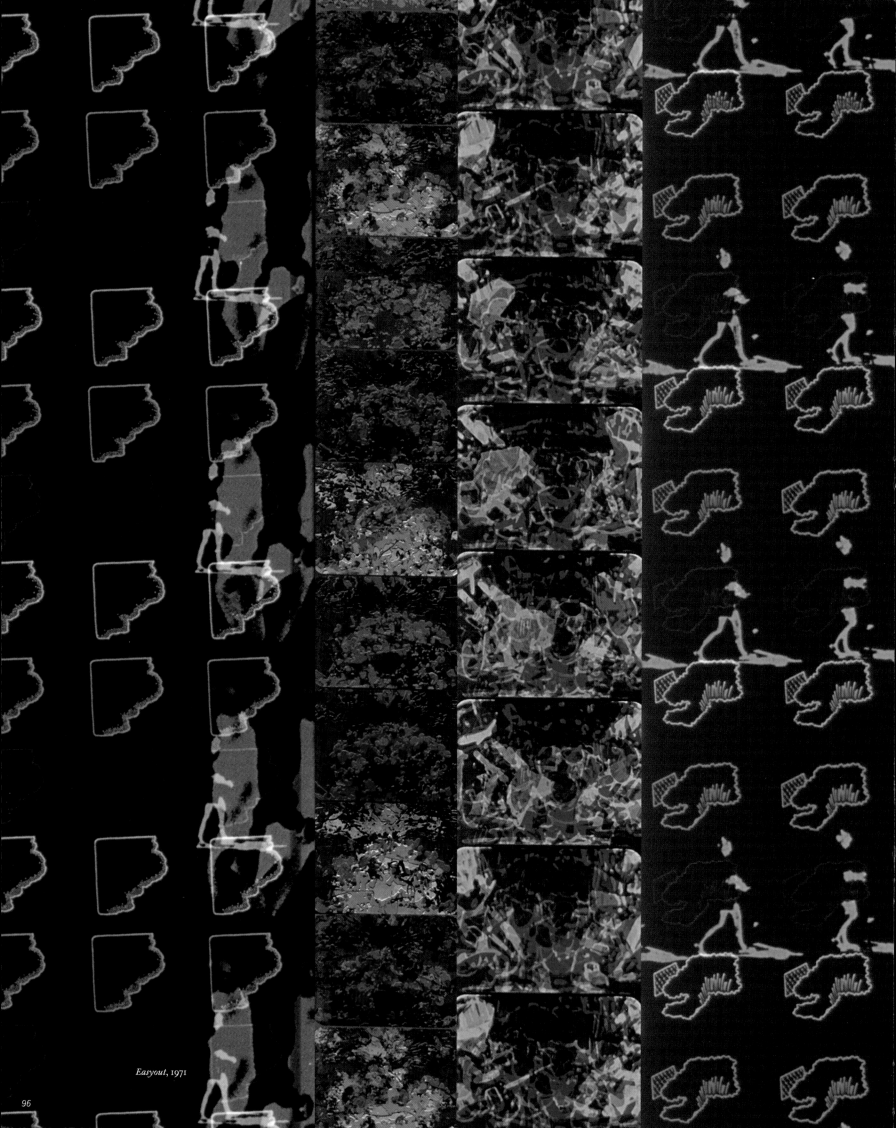

Easyout, 1971

TOP: *Venice Series (4)*, 1960–61
BOTTOM LEFT: *Venice Series (2)*, 1960–61
BOTTOM RIGHT: *Venice Series (6)*, 1960–61

TOP: *Venice Series (5)*, 1960–61
BOTTOM LEFT: *Venice Series (1)*, 1960–61
BOTTOM RIGHT: *Venice Series (3)*, 1960–61

The Decay of Fiction, 2002

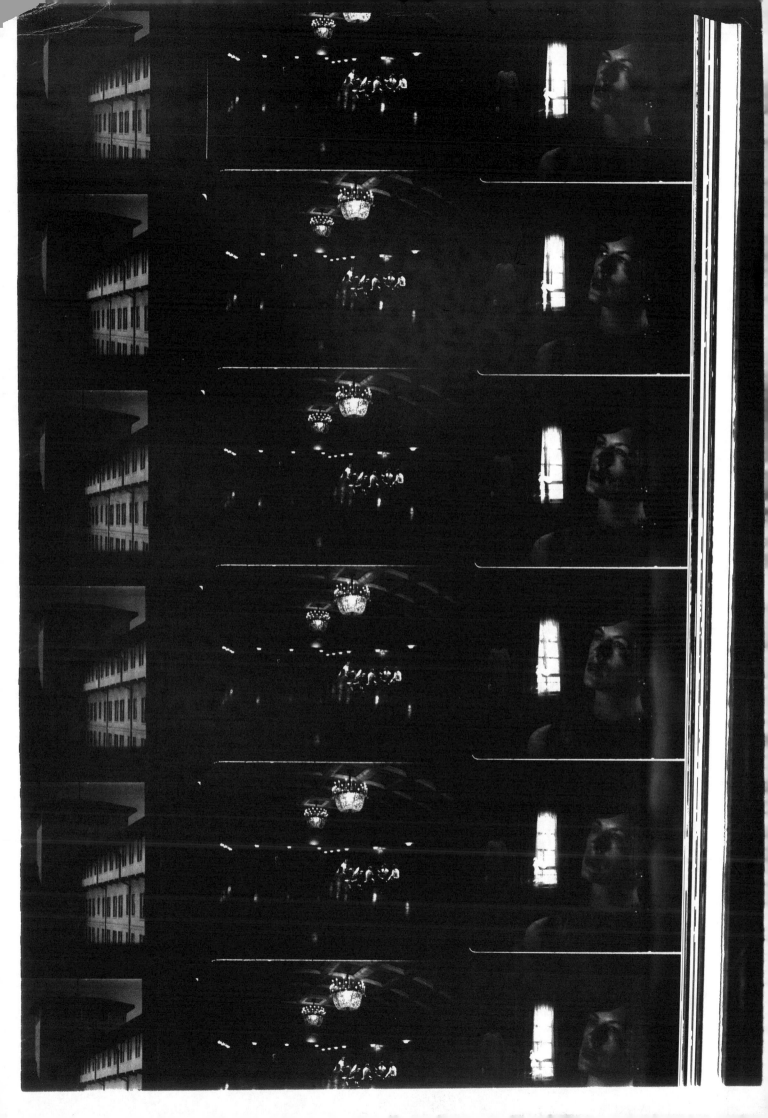

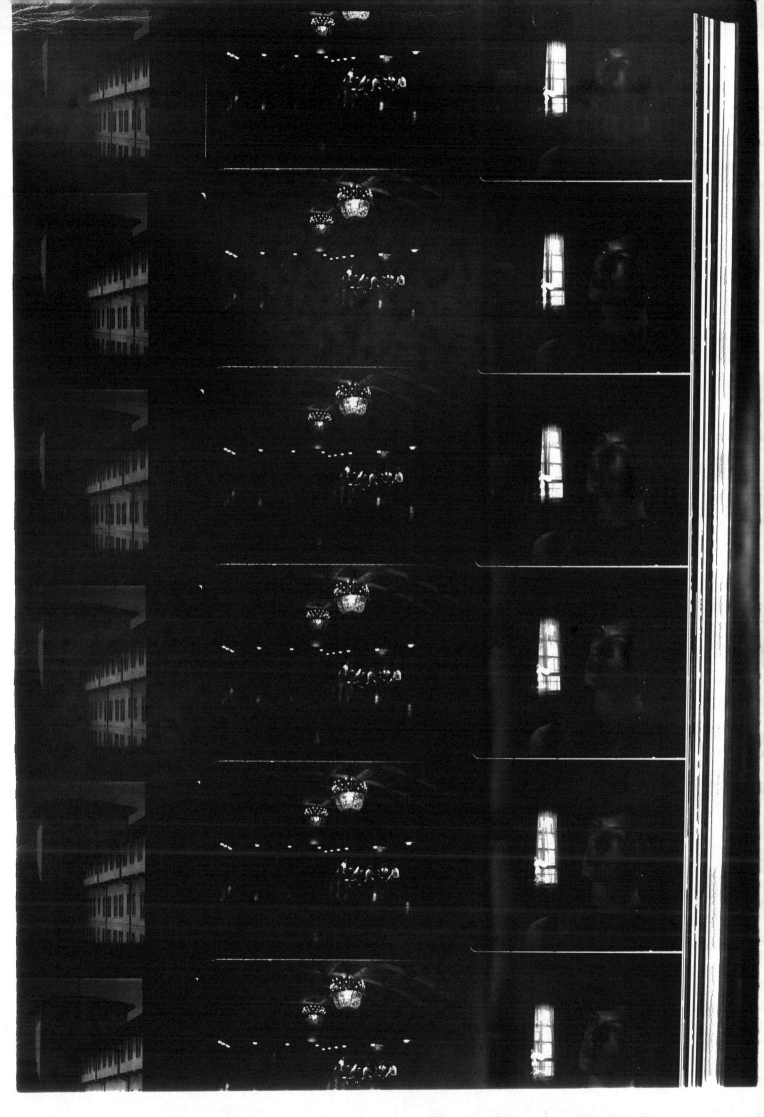

Venice Series (8), 1960–61

See the Native Girls, 1963
Collection of Gaby and Wilhelm Schuermann, Herzogenrath, Germany

Venice Series (7), 1960–61

Dr. Pierce, 2002

Down Wind, 1973

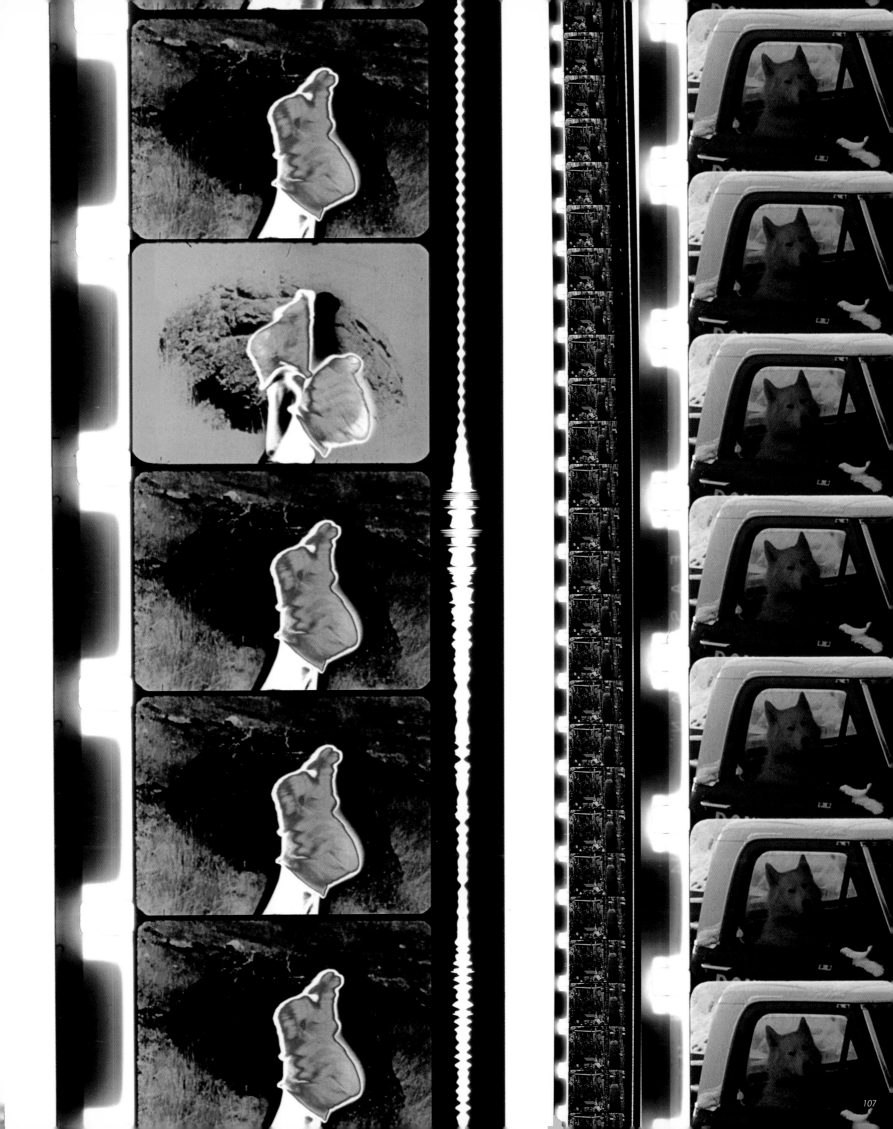

Owens Valley Stack, 1999

Dry Lake Stack, 1999

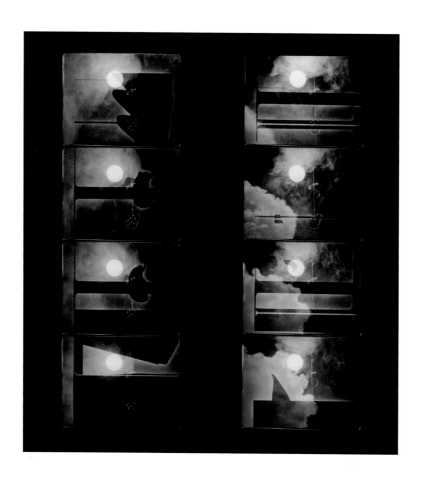

Untitled 1 (excerpts from Trouble in the Image*)*, 1996

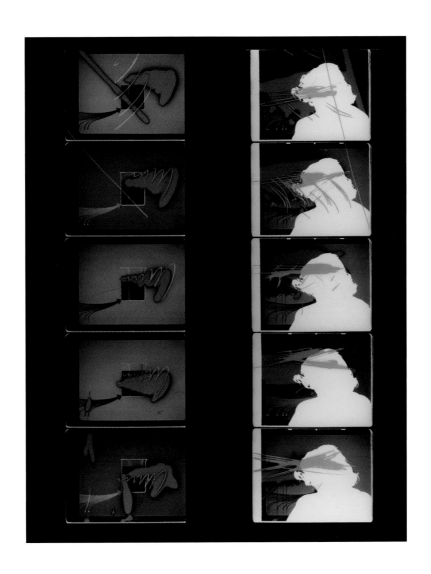

Untitled 4 (excerpts from Trouble in the Image*)*, 1996

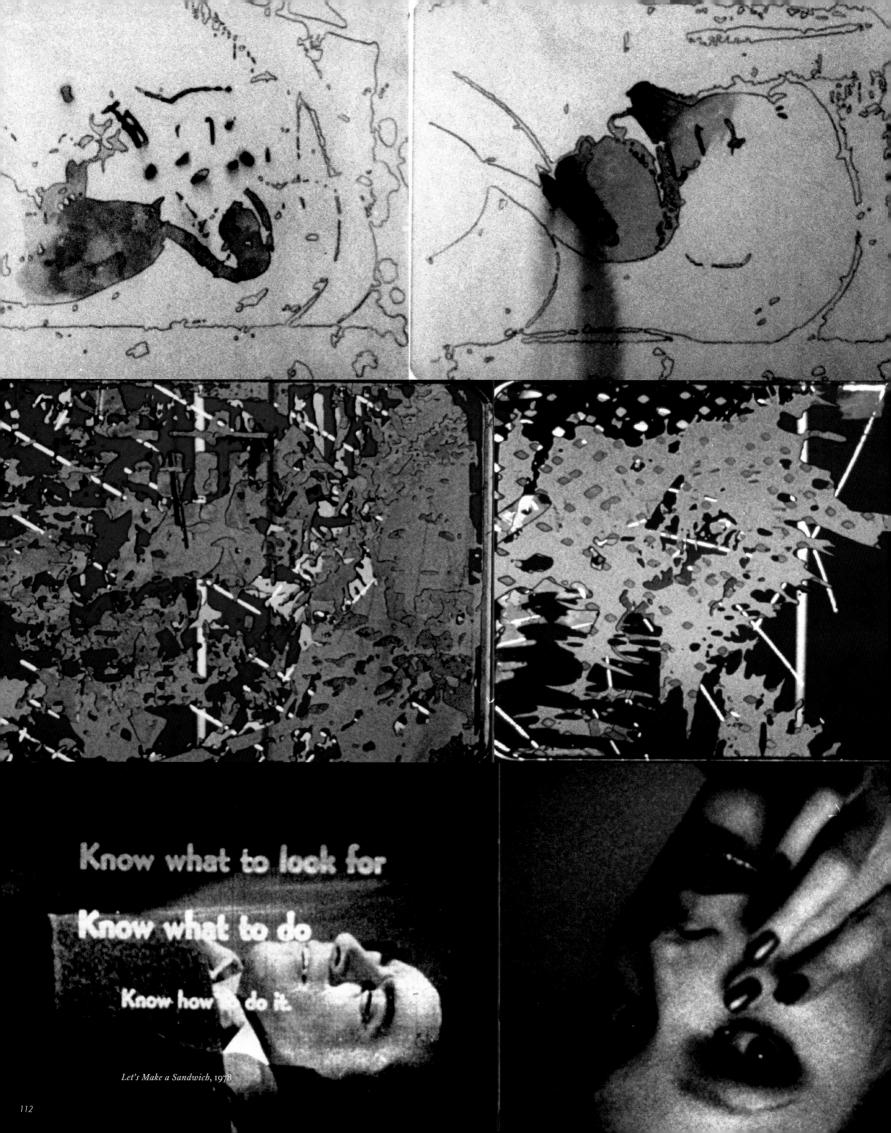

Let's Make a Sandwich, 1978

Let's Make a Sandwich was first presented on a rear-projection screen suspended within a large, dark room. Viewers had access to both sides of the screen, and the film repeated every twenty minutes. The imagery was initially generated by combining many layers of action (from an assortment of personal and industrial footage) without regard to content. The resulting densely figured screen (with its conflicting spaces) may be seen to change with repeat viewing.

THE PERSISTENCE OF PAT O'NEILL
BY HOWARD SINGERMAN

Pat O'Neill has been an internationally known filmmaker since the 1970s, perhaps even since the late 1960s: his *7362* was included in the influential Ann Arbor Film Festival in 1968 and *Runs Good* took first prize there in 1971. He screened films at the Millennium Film Workshop in New York in the early 1970s and had his first retrospective in New York at the FilmForum in 1978. When I mentioned to artists I knew in Los Angeles that I was working on an essay about O'Neill, most of them recognized the name immediately. Some had been his students or acquaintances at the California Institute of the Arts (CalArts), where he taught in the film program from 1970 to 1976. Many had seen his films, or, if they were older, had seen him at Oasis screenings at the Los Angeles Institute of Contemporary Art. When I mentioned my essay on O'Neill to a couple of longtime Los Angeles art dealers, however, they couldn't place the name. While there was, as I recall, a fairly fluid and open relationship between the art world of studio artists and galleries and the community of independent filmmakers in Los Angeles in the 1970s and 1980s, those worlds were not coterminous, and the art world may well have thought of independent film as a subsidiary, or a particular subculture. Though O'Neill has envisioned certain of his films as installations and as multiple or continuous screenings, part of the attraction of film to him very early on was that it could not be owned, that is was "only available for the brief moments when it was on the screen."[1]

Even those artists who recognized O'Neill's name and his achievement were surprised about the aspect of his work I was trying to assay. None knew about his "studio practice," although that might not be quite the right phrase for the photographs, photo-composites, collages, and digital prints he has made for the past three decades: O'Neill hasn't had a traditional artist's studio since 1970. Truth be told, I didn't know until recently that O'Neill has made static works since the early sixties and has an exhibition record that begins shortly after his graduation from the masters program in art at UCLA in 1964. He showed photographs and assemblage early on, had a one-person exhibition of sculpture at Orlando Gallery in Encino in 1966, and was included in a number of group exhibitions at the Esther Robles Gallery on La Cienega between 1966 and 1970, as well as Fidel Danieli's 1968 survey "Plastics: L.A." at Cal State L.A. and Gerald Nordland's "A Plastic Presence," which opened at the Jewish Museum in New York in 1970. I saw my first of O'Neill's static works in person just this fall in the foyer of his house in Pasadena; entitled *Virinia Red* (see page 50), it dates from 1969. Made of polyester laminate on a wood armature and finished in lacquer, the work's materials recall La Cienega Boulevard and the L.A. Finish Fetish, but O'Neill cautions that "compared with the perfec-

Bruce Conner, *A Movie*, 1958

1. From e-mail correspondence with the author, November 5, 2003. Unless otherwise noted, all quotations from Pat O'Neill are drawn from e-mail exchanges that date from November 2003 through January 2004, or from curator Julie Lazar's interview with O'Neill on March 1, 2003.

tion of John McCracken's polyester laminate pieces of Craig Kauffman's vacuum-formed shapes, my work is much cruder, subject to inadvertancies, and at the same time almost representational, in an odd way." Born and raised in Los Angeles, O'Neill shares the car culture that helped to form the palette and material and technological choices—and perhaps the sensibility—of a number of the L.A. plastics artists; he built is own car when he was in high school, he wanted to go to Art Center in automobile design, and took his B.A. at UCLA in product design. A tilting, gently ridged, floor-bound mound, *Virinia Red* is built out of that knowledge, but it is more direct, more process oriented, or at least more "handmade" than a McCracken or a Kauffman. Rather than starting with a given geometry or a readily graspable, designed and profiled form like Kauffman's "thermometers," O'Neill addressed the mold sculpturally, carving away at the plaster with a model-maker's sweep. Looking back, he compares his use of the mold-makers "sweep" with the motion-controlled arc of a camera pan: "Both are the result of rotation about a center. The camera's lens absorbs some version of the world surrounding it, while the sweep lays a shape into plaster which becomes a surface."

O'Neill's sixties sculpture tends toward the biomorphic and eccentric rather than the geometric, toward the assembled or multipartite rather than the unitary, and toward San Francisco or Chicago rather than the L.A. with which we've become familiar. Reviewing Danieli's "Plastics" show in Artforum, Jane Livingston singled out O'Neill to remark on the "unfortunate tendency in L.A. artists working in a latter-day Surrealist and/or Pop vein to imitate earlier styles, particularly in San Francisco and, perhaps, Chicago."[2] She describes the piece that drew her attention, *Safer than Springtime*, as "comprised of three discrete shapes—a lumpy green one, shaped like a pickle, below it a shiny orangeish drum and, spreading over the floor like a pool of blood, a red component." Livingston's geography is essentially correct; the green pickle form rubbed up against the orange drum, is obviously, even adolescently phallic, and the sculpture's slick, plasticized funk sexuality is closer to Jeremy Anderson or Robert Hudson than to Kauffman or McCracken. While O'Neill does speak of Kauffman as an influence, he points not to any specific sculpture, but to an early film, *7362*, and to its flattened symmetry. O'Neill's list of early influences also includes Bruce Conner, "both as an assemblage artist and also a filmmaker"—he saw Conner's *A Movie* shortly after it was completed at the Coronet Theater, one of the few L.A. venues for experimental cinema in the late 1950s and early 1960s—and H.C. Westerman, whose work he first saw at Dilexi Gallery in 1962. Most of O'Neill's mid-sixties sculptures were pedestal top assemblages and in their finish and their trophy verticality,

works like *Carved Clouds* and *War Toy* are closer to Westerman than to either Conner or the L.A. plastics artists. O'Neill began to make assemblages while he was still in high school in the early 1960s, and like any number of sculptors in the fifties and sixties his was a scavenger's aesthetic: "My work at the time involved the inclusion of found, and altered objects, mostly cast iron, aluminum, and zinc consumer product parts from the thirties and forties. These were attached together to form alternative industrial configurations." The scene, and one could say the sensibility, of that work is visible as well in his early photographs. The Atlantic Auto Wrecking series is set in a scrap yard; in it the decaying bodies of 1930s and 1940s automobiles take on the formal gravity of a Henry Moore or the sexualized anthropomorphism of Surrealism. O'Neill's scavenging has also marked his filmmaking, not only in his use of found footage, but also in his experimental, handmade methods of processing and shooting, in his war surplus film stock and jerry-rigged cameras and printers.

Across the 1960s and into the 1970s, O'Neill's visual repertoire included the highly finished pop surrealism and cartoonish sexuality of car and comic subculture; in a review of his 1967 one-person exhibition at Orlando Gallery, William Wilson referred to his sculpture as "Rococo Funk," and the work of a "mad genius hot-rod maker."[3] That description could easily fit the work of other artists, well outside the art world, he was looking at at the time. O'Neill encountered the work of car and motorcycle designer Von Dutch while still in high school and lists the *Zap* comics illustrators Victor Moscoso and Robert Williams as sources as well. Moscoso's metamorphosing Mr. Peanut might be there in the highly finished biology of *L'il Neverbetter* (see page 48). Cast in polyester laminate in sheet acrylic molds in 1969, *L'il Neverbetter* is a sleek, thirty-two-inch long, tri-segmented form, like the body of an ant. O'Neill initially envisioned it as a "free-floating object," one of a series of handheld sculptures, but it turned out too big to be held comfortably and was shelved. The sharp, jagged ended, but equally sleek yellow plastic rods that pierce the body now are a 2003 addition, as is the flattened bottom that allows it to lay flat on the floor, to evoke landscape as well as body. In its early plan as well as in its recent recasting, *L'il Neverbetter* is "full of unprepossessing associative overtones," to borrow Livingston's language. The references to sexual forms or to sexual violence and penetration seem obvious and formalized in a way that very much owes to surrealism after Pop—to "eccentric abstraction" as Lucy Lippard put it.

Speaking in an interview with David E. James about the experiences that were important for him as an artist and filmmaker early on, O'Neill recounted how,

2. Jane Livingston, exhibition review of "Plastics: L.A.," Los Angeles State College, *Artforum* (May 1968), 65.

3. William Wilson, "In the Galleries: Sculptures of Pat O'Neill," *Los Angeles Times*, 13 October 1967, sec. 4.

as a freshman at UCLA, he found finding Salvador Dalí's *Persistence of Memory* in the pages of a *Life* magazine plucked at random from the shelves in the library stacks. He was struck not just by the work but by a recognition, the realization that he had seen it and that same issue of Life in his parents' house as a four-year-old child. O'Neill tells the story in part to suggest his hands-on autodidacticism, or, perhaps, the peculiarity of his formation—"there was no art in my parents' house; there was nobody interested in art or talking about it"—and in part to situate his development away from the school style of UCLA's art department, which favored a figurative abstraction after Matisse: "I tended to be involved with Surrealism and my instructors were appalled."[4] One can understand why; from their point of view, Dalí's version of Surrealism represented middle-brow taste at best, and its appearance in *Life* in 1945 would have been proof of the surrender of Surrealism to popular culture early on. Perhaps O'Neill's attraction to pictorial Surrealism and to Dalí in particular lay in its effect (and not just on his teachers) His *deja-vu* "flash" recalls precisely the displaced temporality of Surrealism itself, the "blasting out of childhood experience" that Adorno makes the central to surrealist practice, or even to what Dalí pictured, Freud's *nachtraglichkeit*, the persistence of memory. That experience requires an already seen, already used, even worn-out image and, perhaps, the kind of laminated, lacquered finish that Dalí shares with photography and with the glossy, photomechanical surface of *Life*. Of all images, the photographic one "wears out most quickly," says Hubert Damisch. "[Photography is] the capturing and restoration of an image already worn beyond repair."[5]

Some of the oldest works in this exhibition are neither films nor sculptures, but photographs made while O'Neill was still a design student at UCLA in 1961 and 1962, taken in and around Venice and what is now Marina del Rey; what they record are worn out or scarred surfaces. "The first shooting I did was in Venice working with the debris of oil wells and the oil industry—the way the tar merged with the sand and the shapes that it made. I was working close up at the time shooting things maybe two feet away or so.... I regret that I didn't step back and document the area I was working in." As O'Neill's recollection suggests, the impulse behind those early photographs was not documentary but formal and symbolic; he remembers, in particular, reading Minor White on Alfred Stieglitz's *Equivalents*, on the possibility that photography could be "metaphorical right from the beginning." The close-up view tends not only to abstract the image, to separate it from recognition, but also to produce the photograph as a flat surface. The act of turning the camera toward the ground or focusing it on a wall closes off deep space and

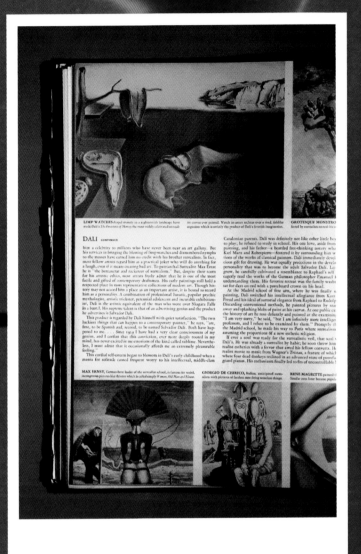

Salvador Dalí, *The Persistence of Memory*, reprinted in *Life*, September 24, 1945

4. David E. James, "An Interview with Pat O'Neill," *Millennium Film Journal*, nos. 30/31 (Fall 1997); available on-line at http://www.mfj-online.org/journalPages/MFJ30%2C31/ DJamesInterview.html.
5. Hubert Damisch, "Notes for a Phenomenology of the Photographic Image," in *Classic Essays on Photography*, ed. Alan Trachtenberg (New Haven, Conn.: Leete's Island Books, 1980), 290.

situates the image at and as the surface. O'Neill's early photos deny the open, perspectival space of the "world viewed," Stanley Cavell's description of photography's usual scene, its automatic cut in the continuous space of the world. They look instead like, and to, abstract paintings, bordered areas of tone and texture that take their frames not as a cut in the world but as a formal limit. O'Neill took his cues and the photographs' flattened focus from photographers like White, Frederick Sommer, and Clarence Laughlin, but his vision is not as lyrical or as rustic as White's nor as gothic as Laughlin's. In its urbanism, it is closer in the early photographs to Aaron Siskind's New York School, but L.A. in the early sixties wasn't as formal a setting, and O'Neill was already interested in its popular, sun-flattened projection of surrealist desire. The walls O'Neill records in *Untitled (25er)*, (1965) (see page 30) or S*ee the Native Girls* (1963) (see page 103) are sign-painted and graffitied, already caught up in L.A.'s peculiar conjunction of sexuality, stilled motion, and the worn-out new.

O'Neill has made photographs throughout his four-decade career, not necessarily and not often as finished works but as visual studies; they appear as stills and backdrops in a number of the films, and as a central component, a setting, for many of the recent digital prints. He describes the process this way: "I photograph irregularly, usually taking several rolls in the course of a week and then none for months. I rarely make pictures with a particular final result in mind, but rather take pictures that are incomplete in themselves, that ask to be altered in some way. After some years of doing this, a considerable library has accumulated." Despite his regret that he didn't step back or look up in those early Venice photographs, his distance, even in his most recent photographs, is formal and compositional rather than perspectival or documentary. His photographs at the Ambassador Hotel, taken during the making of *The Decay of Fiction*, look down on its terraces and patios from above or, in *Untitled (Phone Boxes)* (1993) (see page 188), use its architectural grid to organize and flatten his composition. *Patty (Car with Graffiti)* (1990) (see page 130), returns to the scene, or at least the scenario, of *25er*. In the earlier, black-and-white image, the top half of a late model car is situated parallel to the picture plane and to a wall pentimentoed with an old advertisement for a soda fountain, part visible through whitewash, part still strong black silhouette. In the later image the camera looks down rather than head on: the car in the lower third of the picture is seen almost in full but it is far from whole. Instead it is wrecked and blown open and covered with graffiti that spills across its doors and hood onto the wall that rises behind it. O'Neill hasn't become a documentarian, but something like a history is told in the difference between the two images, by a kind of montage, or conversation.

As O'Neill says, "there is a dialogue between me at 64 and me at 24." Works like *L'il Neverbetter* or the Venice series might seem some distance from the visual and thematic sophistication of the recent films like *The Decay of Fiction* or *Water and Power*, but there are links and visual traces of the early works in the later ones. In some cases, the dialogue O'Neill speaks of has been quite direct and physical: *Virinia Red* and *L'il Neverbetter* are both dated 1969–2003, and both bear the marks of their reencounter. O'Neill cut away the flat bottom of the piece now called *Virinia Red* and destroyed its axial symmetry; he made its stance less solid and its identity as well. Originally untitled, it was named *Untitled (Mound)* when O'Neill returned to it, and it was briefly retitled *Sinking Monument To...* before it received its current name. The most obvious scars from O'Neill's return to the work are those on its sanded away surface, which was initially striped in blue, yellow, and tangerine, a color scheme that once again suggests L.A. in the 1960s and that gave the piece, when he returned to it, a "time-capsule quality." That is, it marked for him a relationship he once had to a particular historical moment, now seen in connection to an oeuvre that has continued in other directions. O'Neill sanded *Virinia Red*'s lacquer finish back along the ridges to reveal a kind of archaeology of its painting and of his working methods. "Working on cars, I was interested in the way sanding revealed successive coats of paint, and the way a variable in the underlying surface would appear as a contour map rendered in rings or stripes of color. Depending on how the paint is applied and abraded, a range of phenomena appear and can be controlled to a degree. Thus a painted surface can be curiously atmospheric, even photographic, in its gradations and interruptions." The space O'Neill has opened up in *Virinia Red* is not an interior or a depth, but a layering of surfaces, like those of automobile paint or of emulsion on film, or of strips of film through the optical printer, where images embed themselves in the spaces and contours of open surfaces left in others. As a number of critics have pointed out, the title of O'Neill's film *Let's Make a Sandwich* refers not only to one of the pieces of found footage that make up the film, but to the process of its making, to the layers and sandwiching of the image. That parallel physical surface and his artisanal production of it might link all of O'Neill's work across media and position it as well toward the graphic—the flattening contour line of the cut out—and to collage, both in its cut and its combination as its dominant term.

I am far from the first to situate O'Neill's sensibility around the surface and its craft. There has been a tendency for those who write about art, at least since the 1960s, to separate the handmade from the crafted. The handmade has come to describe the often deliberately unskilled, ersatz making of a kind of open, needy work. Skilled craft work, in contrast, is finished, closed off to the viewer and seen only be from the outside. O'Neill is familiar with that criticism, which appears even in very supportive reviews: discussing *The Decay of Fiction* in the *Village Voice*, J. Hoberman wrote that, "like all of O'Neill's films, it's magically accomplished. (Too much so, perhaps: The muscular craft sometimes polishes the emotional content to a very fine sheen.)"[6] Writing on *Saugus Series* a decade earlier, Grahame Weinbren and Christine Noll Brinckmann argued against the already common criticism that O'Neill's "films consist only of their surface; that they are 'visual' films," even as they acknowledged that he "presents a surface that is deceptively smooth, often conventionally beautiful (in that its subject is beautiful) and of incomparable cinematic technique."[7] Their argument was that O'Neill's flattened surfaces were active and intentional productions, that surfaceness as such has to be achieved, even represented. They quote Stanley Cavell, who, writing on modernist painting at about the same moment that O'Neill was its pupil, asserted, "phenomenologically the idea of flatness is either an idea of transparency or outline." Weinbren and Brinckmann add the category of the silhouette, or they take it as one of the implications of Cavell's argument; it is the filled-in area of the outline. Together these are the terms of collage: cutting out, filling in, seeing through, particularly the sense of seeing through a surface, an aperture, or a screen. And as O'Neill points out, they are there as well in the outlined, abraded surfaces that run along the ridges of *Virinia Red*.

O'Neill stopped making sculpture in 1970 when he began to teach at CalArts and gave up the studio he shared with Carl Cheng. Two small photomontages produced in 1974, *Untitled* (*Marble*) (see page 138) and *Untitled* (*Fish*) (see page 139), seem some distance from the concerns and the vocabulary—or at least the scale and physicality—of those earlier works. But O'Neill talks about the way the combined images work within the surface as though he was talking about assemblage, assessing their allusionistic effects as if they had physical weight. The composites, in retrospect, resemble the sculptures in the "way that the parts tended to talk to one another. Each one tended to erase the dominance of the other, in the sense that you had to hold more than one thing in your mind at a time." The pictures are wet composites, made in the darkroom; the source images are separate negatives exposed onto a single photographic single surface, and O'Neill links his experiments with the process to the attractions of late-Surrealist photography, to Frederick Sommer's superimpositions and Jerry Uelsmann's multiple composites. But in the combination of images on the surface and the process of weighing and holding

them there, there is also a clear link to the films O'Neill had begun to make in the early 1960s and his approach to making them. The picture's compositions are gridded and formalized; the aquarium display that fills in over a used-car lot and the classical statuary on the British Museum wall that rises above an old, inverted car hood in the Mexican desert, flatten the space of the photographs and push it horizontally as though across a screen. The images fill the rectangle the way film does and, at least in *Untitled* (*Fish*), one could take the line-up of cars and spectators below an expansive screen as a figure for film O'Neill has remarked that the influence runs both ways: his film work is indebted to his still photography. Since at least *Runs Good* in 1970, he has assembled found, usually narrative, and certainly "moving picture," footage, but he most often situates those filmed movements within a still frame, as an inset or episode. "My interest in the relationship between elements in static shots has led me to make films that either have no cuts, or that have pauses between shots"—as though each shot sets up another picture and announces another relationship.

Perhaps the early question for O'Neill in both film and photography was how to hold two images together. It began as a literal or experiential question. In 1963, O'Neill and his collaborator, fellow UCLA student Bob Abel, wanted to shoot their first film, *By the Sea*, on a high-contrast stock that would generalize and flatten the forms, an effect O'Neill had already come to in his still photography; something equivalent to the graphic flatness and emotional blankness of *Untitled* (*Fun*) (see page 30), a picture taken that same year in an abandoned amusement park in San Francisco. The stock they found was a relatively obscure 35mm version of a graphic design sheet film that O'Neill and Abel slit into 16mm and sprocketed; their initial contact printer was equally jerry-rigged, a Bolex running two strips of film and a light bulb. "I could see that if you had a device to hold an image steady in the gate the world would be wide open to you, you could do film work or single images in the same format." That world would be constructed and composited rather than viewed straight on.

The device existed, of course, and O'Neill began to work with an optical printer on his own films work shortly thereafter; the machinery became his livelihood by the mid-1970s and he began to produce still images that way as well. "I would be running film for a project of my own or for someone else and I would take a little bit of the leader at the end and do a composition spontaneously on the printer and some of those turned out to be some of those composites that I did." The composited images of the 1980s, works like *Punch*

6. J. Hoberman, "They Aim to Please," *Village Voice*, 9–15 October 2002.
7. Grahame Weinbren and Christine Noll Brinckmann, "Selective Transparencies: Pat O'Neill's Recent Films," *Millennium Film Journal*, no. 6 (Spring 1980): 53–55.

Me In (1984) (see page 60), or *Seated Coil* (1985) (see page 177), are not exactly film stills, but, as the framing and sprocketing along their edges suggest, they are produced on motion picture stock and begin as single film frames. O'Neill collected passing, almost inadvertent, visual material—fragments of advertising, commercial paint chips, doodles on napkins, and the like—and photographed them, one frame at a time, on a lightbox on an animation stand. These images and shapes were then used to mask and divide the image on a frame that contained still other photographic imagery. "I was never able to see a composition until it was completed in its entirety, and every variable I was using would have to be tested as to exposure and color balance in advance." *Punch Me In* is, O'Neill suggests, an essay on the surface: "essentially it's four quadrants that are each made out of the same sort of ingredients, which are found diagrams and some tape and some spontaneous paint application that was made into a xerox and then copied. So everything that's added is referring to the surface: it's flat stuff."

The lightbox on which *Punch Me In* was photographed, and the flatness it asserted, are thematized by the heavy frames and glass of a series of collages O'Neill produced from the mid-1970s to early 1980s. Made of ripped down 2 x 4s, a cut more closely linked to construction rather than to fine-art frames, these frames suggest quite literal windows, and were originally intended to act that way; O'Neill planned to exhibit them in front of lightboxes or in openings in the gallery wall. The collages are not matted or backed, but suspended, sandwiched between two panes of glass, a reference not only to windows but to the "gate" of a camera or projector or an optical printer, open to light on either side. Where O'Neill's film work often suggests the influence and presence of still photography, these heavily framed collages seem the inverse, an attempt to put film at the center of a studio practice in a way that would reference both the artisanal making of the sculpture and the hand processing of film. Here film sets the questions and some of what is sandwiched between the panes of glass, particularly in the earlier pieces such as *Untitled (Head/Tail Strips)* (1974) (see page 153) and *Untitled (Ruled/Scratched)* (1975) (see page 159) is film itself. In *Head/Tail Strips* O'Neill presents a different sort of found footage; film that lies, so to speak, outside the work, or at least outside the process of recording and of the lens: "In the course of doing commercial film work I handled hundreds of rolls a month and sometimes when I was throwing them out I would break off the leaders because I found them intriguing in the fact that they were never the same twice. Various kinds of odd color tints got into them—it's accidental light that gets on the film in the lab—and occasionally there would be a little bit of picture somewhere." O'Neill notes that in the 1960s or early 1970s, both Austrian experimental filmmaker Peter Kubelka and the late New York filmmaker Paul Sharits exhibited film as a sculptural object (or in the case of Sharits's *Frozen Film Frames*, sandwiched in Plexiglas, one could argue, as painting) but each to a different end. Kubelka pinned entire 35mm films to the museum or gallery wall, or across its windows as a way to insist on their materiality and his systemic, linear image production. Kubelka's description of "film [as] a transparent sculpture," seems to fit O'Neill's framed and mounted leader, but the kind of sculpture it is might be *objet trouvé*: film as found object. They are not about the film as a single object or system so much as they are about film as a surface and as an incident or moment.

The paper works sandwiched between glass—*Untitled (Camera)* (see page 155), *Untitled (China/Food)* (see page 158), *Untitled (Cathedral)* (see page 157), all from the early 1980s—are more recognizably collages, *papier collés*. But they appear here under the conditions of film, again not just under glass, but between glass, and, in the case of *Untitled (Torn Portrait)* (see page 156), open like film in the projector or the optical printer to both sides. Even those works that aren't so obviously or physical open and, in that sense, transparent, have no ground. Unlike collages built up on board or a rectilinear paper ground, there is no support, no overall field to contain them or to stop them from the back. They are amalgamations of two or three things that joint—a rococo church, a encyclopedia illustration or an oak leaf, and a image of the demolition of the old Los Angeles Children's Hospital in *Cathedral*; a Spam dinner and a sheet from a Chinese medical atlas in *China/Food*. Floated and joined in the glass, they become overall sculptural shapes or exterior forms as well as juxtaposed images. Without the ground, the sandwiching and layering is even more obvious, more physical, as is the flatness of the material, once again: "everything that's added is referring to the surface: it's flat stuff."

Writing in 1978 on the composition of O'Neill's film space in the *Saugus Series*, Weinbren argued that "one cannot help reading the objects in [O'Neill's] image to be situated in spatial relations to the plane of the image that is supposedly flat and non-illusionistic."[8] The rudimentary shape at the center of *Camera*, a 1983 collage, first appears in the *Saugus Series* and it acts, as Weinbren suggests, as an ambiguous marker of space in relation to the flattened, layered surface. The simple, graphic perspective drawing—one box set atop another larger one, and set obliquely to the implied surface—both designates space and in its hard black line, flattens it, registers it as a representation or designation. The torn edge of its paper surface both opens up a space, a kind of

8. Grahame Weinbren, "Six Filmmakers and an Ideal of Composition," *Millennium Film Journal*, no. 3 (Winter/Spring 1979): 53.

aperture in the feathered French endpaper, and asserts its material flatness. The stacked boxes might be what gives the collage its name; the shape might be taken as rudimentary camera lens or bellows and back. It isn't one, of course; rather it is an assignment, an exercise from a mechanical drawing textbook. O'Neill speaks of seeing such typeforms through the lens of Robert Morris or Tony Smith: "Each of them was a proposal for an object and you could think of it as something very large.... It seemed to be the archetype for a way of thinking that tends to have straight lines and they tend to be at right angles." O'Neill has an affection for the didactic, particularly the didactic that is just past—see for example the instructional footage of *Let's Make a Sandwich*—as well as for the drawn, the graphic line that is also situated outside and before current technology. *Camera* makes reference to a number of just such outmoded forms: the hardline drawing of architectural drafting and its teaching by typeforms have long been replaced by CAD; handmade feathered endpapers are now produced photographically, if at all; and (at least in the headlines) the books that such endpapers might enclose are threatened by the digital, as are the optics of the camera. The drawing on which the endpaper sits also has an oddly anachronistic feel, as if it has recorded too much time; such drawings are, for O'Neill, the record of time spent, even time wasted, and of waiting.

Done in meetings and waiting rooms, in the midst of long phone conversations or on airplanes, O'Neill refers to these drawings as "jailhouse" drawings: records of "a condition of captivity and passivity." They are in some sense just doodles—8 1/2 x 11 sheets of paper and a pencil or a ballpoint pen—but they were a significant portion of his artistic output in the 1980s, after he had left CalArts and after the success of the *Star Wars* films for which his studio, Lookout Mountain, had done a good deal of special effects work. "I began to realize that each one of these was like a little specimen, like a medical test of some kind to show what was going on in my mind." They are heir to Surrealist automatism and, in their "all-over" composition, they have a family resemblance to its history. They are slower, though, and more intricate and incidental; as O'Neill explains they do without "not only representation, but also gestural movement—they are the result of small wrist and finger movements, such as might be done in a small space." O'Neill soon began to recognize the meeting room drawings as an art practice and to formalize and set rules for their making. "The mark-making process is carried on with the page being rotated 90 degrees from time to time. Marks are laid down without preconception, but once a mark has been made, it is never obscured by other marks." Rotating the page is a way of keeping questions of gravity and orientation, depth, and resemblance open. In any given passage O'Neill's drawing responds to its local position and its current orientation, but by regularly rotating the image, he is able to build a "surface that has no defined point of entry." "The surface is made up of interlocking passages (lines, shapes, gradations, textures) which are usually tethered to representation and which seem to elicit an effort on the part of the viewer to interpret them as such... to 'see' things that were not consciously depicted." "Perhaps," he continues, "the drawing is training us in a particular mode of experiencing. When we are in this mode we are momentarily removed from our usual on-the-ground state of mind."

"On the ground" is probably the operative phrase. There is something about the drawings that suggests topography and an aerial view: we are not viewing a vertical image opposite us but something horizontal and spread out, which is the aspect O'Neill had on them to begin with. They were made horizontally, on the plane surface of graphics and writing, rather than vertically, like a painting on an easel or wall. They belong, in Walter Benjamin's words, to the "cross-section" of graphic art, rather than the "longitudinal section of painting:" "The longitudinal section seems representational; it somehow contains the objects. The cross-section seems symbolic; it contains signs." Benjamin's "sign" is complex; it is not only linear but also inscribed or impressed into the surfaces that it takes up as background. It designates among other things, a relationship between line and the ground on which it sits. A painting, Benjamin insists, "has no background," but "the graphic line marks out the area and so defines it by attaching itself to it as its background.... The graphic line can exist only against this background, so that a drawing that completed covered its background would cease to be a drawing."[9] The all-overness of O'Neill's earliest drawings comes close to a fullness that for Benjamin might mean they were no longer drawings, but even these early works produce a surface that folds and ripples, grows denser or more open. It isn't layered physically like the collages or optically like *Punch Me In*. Rather, the surface is connective, rhizomatic, or metonymic in its construction; things are placed not within or beneath one another but against and adjacent.

The drawings from the 1980s are closely grained in their incident and more continuous and all-over in their effect. They seem to have been structured in quadrants that suggest or perhaps record O'Neill's practice of turning them to keep them from having a top and bottom, from going vertical, one could say. The more recent drawings, most of which date from 1995–96, are more gestural and denser at the center, some proceeding from the center out rather

9. Walter Benjamin, "Painting and Graphic Arts" and "Painting, or Signs and Marks," in Marcus Bullock and Michael W. Jennings, eds., *Walter Benjamin: Selected Writings*, vol. 1, 1913–1926 (Cambridge, Mass.: Harvard University Press, 1996), 82–86.

than from the edges in. The overall space is tenser and more active, and there is a new vocabulary of larger marks—designed lines that act in relation to one another above the plane of the drawing, and the surface of something like landscape. The lines snake across that landscape like earthworks or inscriptions, or the tire tracks on the burned ground of the Central Valley's Kettleman Junction, an image that appears in O'Neill's *Anvil Point*. But in their energetic motion and their slight bulbousness—coils, sproings—they point to sources not so much in the land as on the graphic page. Like O'Neill's sculptural work of the 1960s, their surrealism is more popular, and more trippy, than orthodox or heroic. It is these lines that suggest the linear sound effects of animated cartoons or the metamorphosing figures of Moscoso's *Zap* or the thorny, outlined, and chromed calligraphy of Robert Williams, or the Kelly/Mouse studios. O'Neill recalls working in the 1970s on sequences of Max Fleischer's "Betty Boop" cartoons on a Moviola with the late artist and designer Martin Muller (who as Neon Park designed album covers for the Mothers of Invention and Little Feat). The process, he says, was one of "obliterating the characters and retaining the rhythms, shapes, and line quality," which seems a very good description of how those images appear in the drawings as well.

Slow, intricate, and involved, the drawings point to O'Neill's considerable facility and, in their automatism, to the hand itself as, in Henri Focillon's words, "an organ of knowledge."[10] The drawings are, O'Neill points out somewhat sardonically, necessarily small scale and deliberately "green:" "they result in an absolute minimum of expense and almost no environmental harm. Twenty years work could be done for less than a dollar. This may eventually be necessary." In all these ways, they seem nearly the opposite of the large digital images he began to produce in the late 1990s. O'Neill had used a digital scanner and printer from the late 1980s as a way to greatly enlarge the images he made on film stock in the optical printer It was only later, around 1996 that he reluctantly came to use the computer to process images. The digitally manipulated image might seem an odd choice for O'Neill, since both his artistic output and his commercial work are known for their painstaking, hands-on craft, and for the optical and the analogue. One could think of the digital as a kind of de-skilling; certainly it made the kinds of effects O'Neill once produced commercially obsolete and his embrace of it as an artistic tool is, perhaps, somewhat ironic. Usually those arts that intensify the experience of the manual and of craft rely on outmoded forms of reproductive technology: the forms of fine art printmaking, for example—etching, engraving, and lithography—were once modes of mass reproduction.

Neon Park's artwork for album cover, Frank Zappa's *Weasels Ripped My Flesh*
Collection of Pat O'Neill

10. Henri Focillon, *The Life of Forms in Art* (New York: Zone Books, 1989), 166.

O'Neill seems to work this ironic disjuncture between new media and the passé quite deliberately. There is something not so much nostalgic—a term he would dismiss, in any event—as archaic in his digital images, a feeling that emerges in part because the digital has allowed him to focus his attention rather specifically on the graphic line that formed the basic vocabulary of an earlier, prephotographic mode of spatial representation and mechanical reproduction. What O'Neill scavenges now are images that date from the "period when books were illustrated with line cuts made by hand by illustrators, rather than with photographs which have been converted by use of the halftone screen." In those illustrations, light-dark contrast and space are produced by a line that follows contour or parallels it and that in some sense belongs or adheres to the object represented. The half-tone, in contrast, screens the object; it belongs to a different kind of layering. Not Benjamin's line, but a mark above the surface and continuous with it. O'Neill's choice of line illustrations is, then, a conscious eschewal of another art history, one of reproduction that took the screened photograph and what O'Neill calls its "halftone buzz" as its image, an artistic lineage that would run from Warhol and Lichtenstein to Sigmar Polke.

In their use of line illustration and their juxtaposition of line art from a number of different sources and different narratives, the digital prints O'Neill has produced over the past three or four years (images like *Downdraft* [1998, see pages 78–79] or *Dr. Pierce* [2002, see page 105] or *Rocky Grant, Windows* [2002, see page 34]) bear a strong resemblance to Max Ernst's *La Femme 100 Tetes*. Indeed, O'Neill's sources and methods are situated quite closely to where German critic and theorist Theodor Adorno found Max Ernst's: "These images derive, partly literally and partly in spirit, from illustrations of the later nineteenth century, with which the parents of Max Ernst's generation were familiar." The model of all Surrealism is not a symbol or a psychology, Adorno suggests, but an "artistic technique." It is "unquestionably the montage."

One must therefore trace the affinity of surrealistic technique for psychoanalysis not to a symbolism of the unconscious, but to the attempt to uncover childhood experiences by blasting them out. What surrealism adds to the pictorial rendering of the world of things is what we lost after childhood: when we were children those illustrations, already archaic, must have jumped out at us, just as the surrealistic pictures do now.... [T]he archaic contributes to this effect. As to modernity, there is a paradox in that, although already under the spell of the uniformity of mass production, it still has a history. This paradox alienates it and becomes in the "Children's Pictures for Moderns" the expression of a subjectivity that grown strange to itself.[11]

The scene Adorno describes repeats the story O'Neill tells of his encounter with Dalí in the pages of *Life*, a story marked, like montage, by the temporal and spatial displacement of the image. Dalí's *Persistence* appears in the library as, at once, the image of an old popular culture, an already aging modernity, and a forgotten moment in the life of the subject.

Much of what O'Neill catalogues and combines in his recent digital images comes from found how-to books, manuals, and guides, sources that situate the viewer and the artist, as students or children in the regime of images, or, in most of his examples, of signs. These signs are usually opaque and the knowledge they represent is somehow lost, even if their didacticism is not: "I am," he says, "particularly fond of schematic demonstrations: graphs of all kinds, charts, blueprints, maps, engineering drawings." The mechanical drafting models that appeared early on in the *Saugus Series* and *Camera* are supplemented in digital composites like *Downdraft* by a extensive array of didactic figures: diagrams of automobile engines, guides to masonry patterns and architectural forms, and a sheaf of botanical, entomological, and biological illustrations. *Snake is on the Right* (2003) (see pages 54–55) layers a number of borrowed representational vocabularies: on the left side, in a detail lifted from an 1880s textbook, folds of fabric and the roughened surface of tree bark are delineated with a line that follows fluidly along those intricate surfaces and differentiates their textures; on the right side, in an engraving taken whole from a German zoology text dated 1907, the snake named in the title is tightly rendered, drawn with a line that repeats its patterns, but situated in a far more open space drawn in a staccato, even mechanical line. Over them both is a field of black and gray symbols, like graphic semaphore; despite their seeming, or at least contextual, opacity and archaism, they are of quite recent vintage. Their source is a catalogue of "wipes," the set of mattes and movements commercial optical houses use to transit from one shot or scene to another—that is, to conceal and reveal an image, which is what they do here.

To the line art that he finds in thrift store books and old newspaper clippings, O'Neill has added his own jailhouse drawings. Digitized, the drawings can be sampled, reversed, multiplied, and solarized, and they have become an important part of the recycled material out of which composite images are made. Often O'Neill presents them—albeit greatly transformed—on their own or as the central image, using the digital technology to join and intertwine the surfaces of existing drawings, not just enlarging them but continuing their surfaces across other surfaces or burying them one beneath another. In *Sweet Pea* (2002) (see page 37), the surface is thick and crowded;

11. Theodor W. Adorno, "Looking Back on Surrealism," in *The Idea of the Modern in Literature and the Arts*, ed. Irving Howe (New York: Horizon Press, 1967), 222.

O'Neill's own drawing shares the space with an electrical diagram and a botanical illustration—the sweet pea of the title from an 1887 manual—but it covers those images and pulls them up into its weaving. The most "abstract expressionist" of O'Neill's images, *Sweet Pea*'s white writing surface clearly invokes Mark Tobey and Paul Klee, and, in its density, finally, Jackson Pollock. O'Neill writes of the piece in terms not unlike those of Pollock or his critics: "everything has to cancel out, to neutralize." He even speaks of being "in" the image, as Pollock famously did, though for O'Neill it means that he's there with us as we look: "I have left [intentional] markers along the trail in some parts and not in others." In *Carpet I* (2003) (see page 184–85) and *Bamboo Action Map* (2003) (see pages 182–83) the drawn field and the sense of the page or ground on which it is inscribed extends laterally from denser to more open. *SD3* (2003) (see page 94) reads as a continuous explosion, a figure that expands vertically from bottom to top across the page, as though in time as well as in space. In a sense, the extension of *SD3* or *Carpet* works like a pan in film, a continuation or elongation of the frame elsewhere, and it follows the kind of lateral motion O'Neill introduced for the first time in his films in *Water and Power*.

O'Neill's digital prints fall into three categories: works whose primary surface is drawing, those whose primary material is line art or the prephotographic, and those that take the photograph as their space, their *mise-en-scène*. The space of the first two categories remains modernist space; flat and layered, it is the space of cubism and montage. It tends to extend laterally, but even in a vertically layered work like *Sweet Pea* or *Bascom's Heart* (2003) (see page 92), depths tend to be tied to the surface; the latter picture seems to owe a debt to Polke in its fabric screens and the scale of its figure. The photographs build a deeper, more atmospheric space, though at times O'Neill has deliberately pulled even that space toward and parallel to the surface; that is the formal task of the rotoscoped figure in *Charley, Studio City* (2002), and the sketched-in stage space in *Earfalls* (2003) (see page 129) that both presents and schematizes its seascape depth. Most of the other photo-based works, particularly those O'Neill groups together as the Performance series, open a space more baroque than modern: a deeper, theatrical, and often diagonal space. A number of his images make clear their art historical debt; their spaces and pictures are quite literally borrowed from the art of the seventeenth century. The sweep of *Costume Figures, Amsterdam* (2002) (see page 147) runs alongside the image of Bartholomeus van der Helst's huge *Company of Captain Roelof Bicker and Lieutenant Jan Michielsz Blaeuw* of 1639, a grand Dutch group portrait of some eight feet high by twenty-four and a half feet

wide. O'Neill's title describes both those members of the company of Captain Bicker that occupy the left side of the image and the enigmatic masked figures that O'Neill positions on the right. Captured in motion, just barely blurred or double exposed, O'Neill's figures are dressed in classical shifts—or maybe just sun dresses—and adorned in what seems like animal masks or beaked bird heads; they hover between the archetypal and the tawdry. The figure is O'Neill himself, and he reappears as a performer, costumed and abstracted, in a number of these photographic composites, in their choreographed processions across the dramatic night expanse of the desert southwest.

The choreography in the Performance series puts the human figure in motion both physically and digitally; the diagonals that move across the desert hills or against the night sky are sometimes the photographic image of multiple performers, but more often the digital or photographic repetition of the same figure turned and moved to figure space. In either case and across all of the images, the figures are convulsed and blurred by motion and held in place by a stark white light against the dark ground. The reference again is to the baroque, and more specifically to Caravaggio or the trope of sharp light amidst deep black that came to be known early on as Caravagesque. The dramatized themes of ritual and performance and the dramatic space of the composite pictures are as tied to O'Neill's recent film practice as the flattened, montaged space of the earlier photographs was tied to his earlier ones. *Water and Power* began to open up a kind of lateral space; it offers in passages—in the interior space of the artist's studio, for example—a kind of diagetic extension that the earlier "still" films, centered on the single image and its disassembly, did not need. And it introduced, as well, the sort of stopped motion recorded in the digital images: the still body whose face becomes a blur of movement. The space and imagery of the Performance series is tied directly to *The Decay of Fiction*, most obviously through the performance figures themselves, who move ritually, if chaotically, through the halls of the Ambassador at the film's climax. O'Neill's use of the human figure as actor rather than incident and his evocation of narrative is new in the Performance prints and *The Decay of Fiction*. In the film, the space his actors seem to demand is opened up not only by pans or tracking shots, but by O'Neill's overall mapping out of the hotel as a stage, a continuous narrative place, and his extension of human movement across that space and in relation to it. O'Neill talks about the emptying out of human presence in his earliest photographs and films, or the generalizing of their presence as design as a way to flatten the space and its emotional charge. The visual materials of the first films and photomontages matter, one could say, only in juxtaposition, only in the sense of discomfort or delayed recognition, the sense that they are *made* strange. The images, monsters, and rituals that O'Neill produces in *The Decay of Fiction*, in contrast, work not by montage but by staging; the meaning belongs to them and their evocations—to the narrative and ritual they suggest. And that brings with it a different sort of space, the dramatized space of interiority and rhetorical action that for O'Neill, it seems, belongs as much to painting or its history as it does to film.

In their scale and space and their insistence on human action, the Performance series prints look quite different from most of O'Neill's previous works, whether in film or on the wall. But there is a way in which these works, too, participate in the dialogue he has posed "between me at 64 and me at 24." O'Neill taught a course at CalArts on filming dance in the early 1970s and the human body in choreographed motion, flattened and mechanized, was the subject early on of *7362*. Beyond that there is an echo of the early sculptures in the thick, blurred human forms in works like *Swordfish I* and *Bastard I*. The foreground figure in *Swordfish I* is O'Neill: "This is my back, it turns into a sculptural object, a vegetable or a pepper." "Think of Edward Weston's curling pepper," he says, but in his own oeuvre one could think of the way in which *Virinia Red* seems to rotate and blur in space, or the way it and *L'il Neverbetter* suggest both landscape and the reclining figure in it. Forms that blur the edge between the human and the vegetal or the sculptural set within a melodramatically lit and perspectively endless landscape space, the Performance prints recall, and perhaps make specific reference to, the Surrealism that O'Neill rediscovered in the UCLA library; his *Persistence of Memory* story has, after all, not just two moments in time but three: the artist at four, the artist at nineteen, and the artist who recounts the story in 1997, in the midst of shooting the choreographed monsters and narrative corridors of *The Decay of Fiction*. In this last moment, Surrealism comes not so much under the sign of sexuality as it does with questions of mortality.

Top: Mark Tobey, *Serpentine*, 1955
Bottom: Frederick Sommer, *Arizona Landscape*, 1943

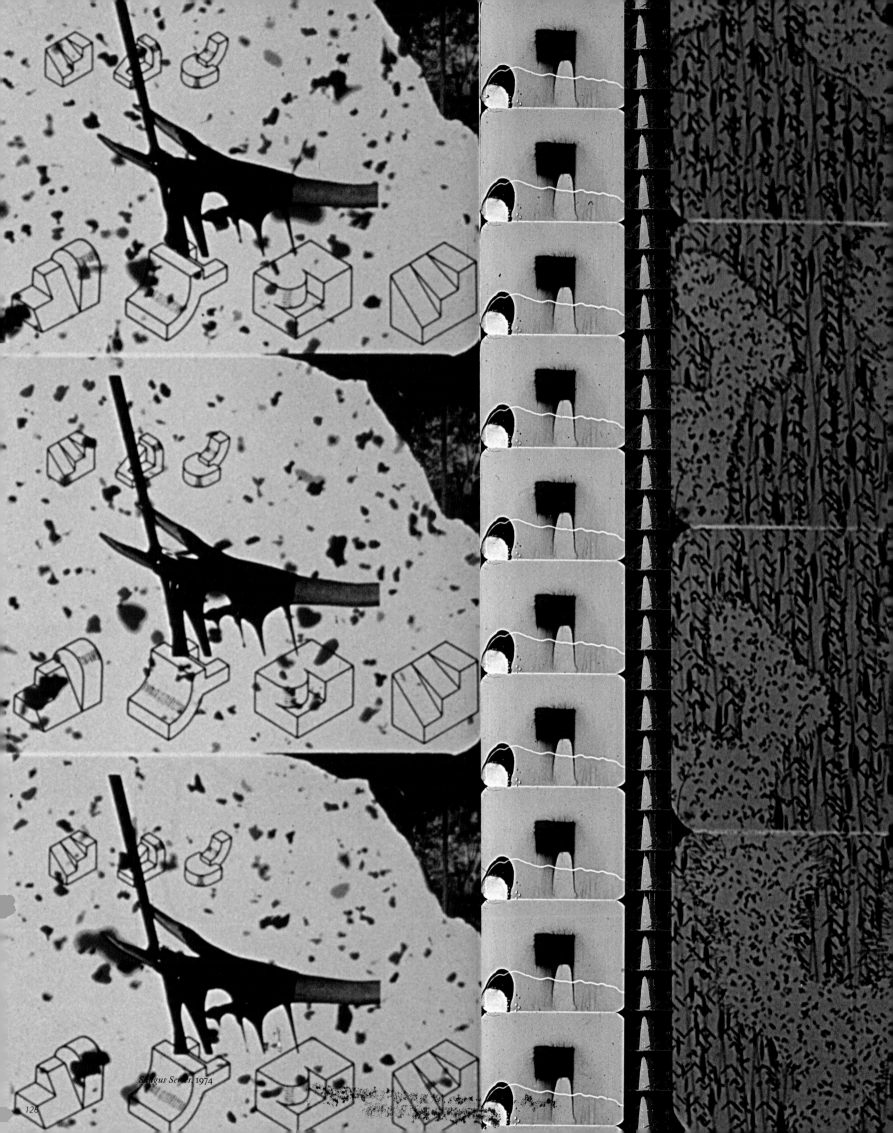

Saugus Series, 1974

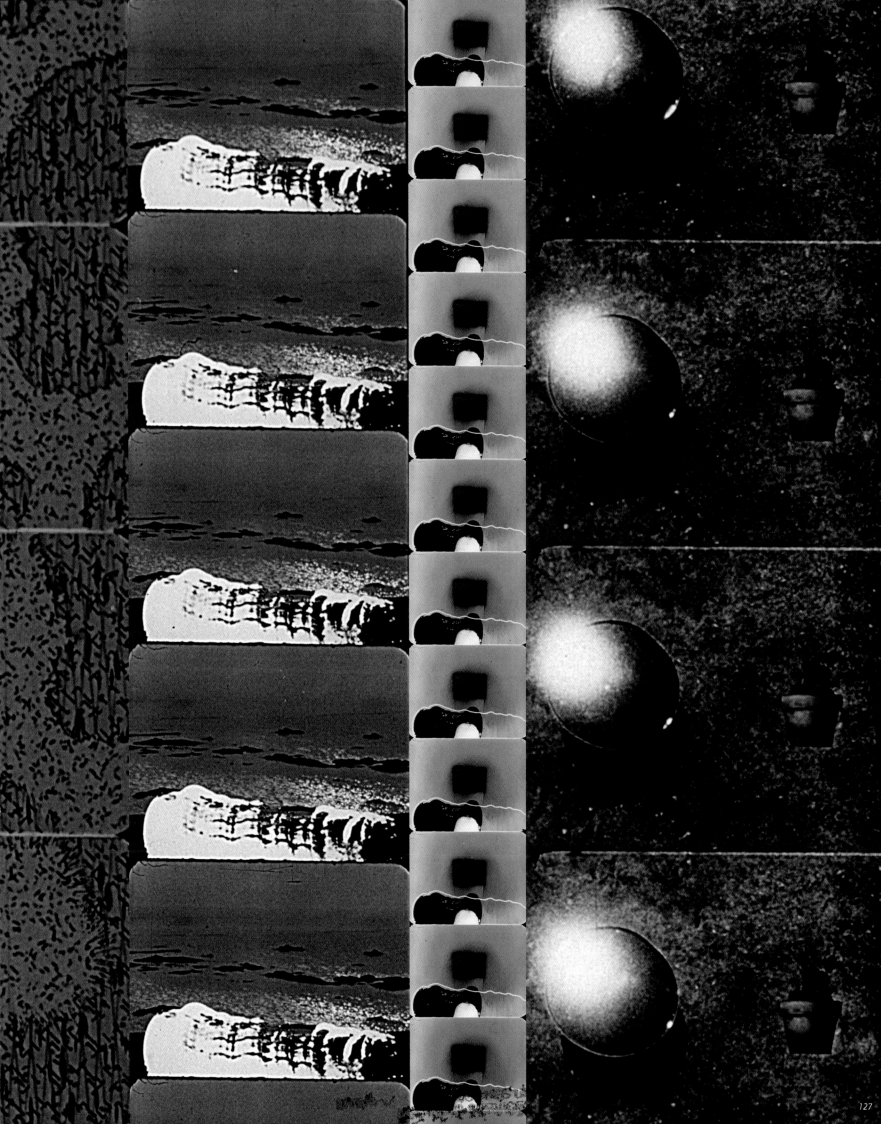

Triumph of Flattery, 1998

Earfalls, 2003

Patty (Car with Graffiti), 1990

Twelve Chairs, 1990

3XXX 21 (Sulfur), 1995

Untitled (Four Piles of Salt), 1990

Mother Loathed (The Bagpipes), 1997

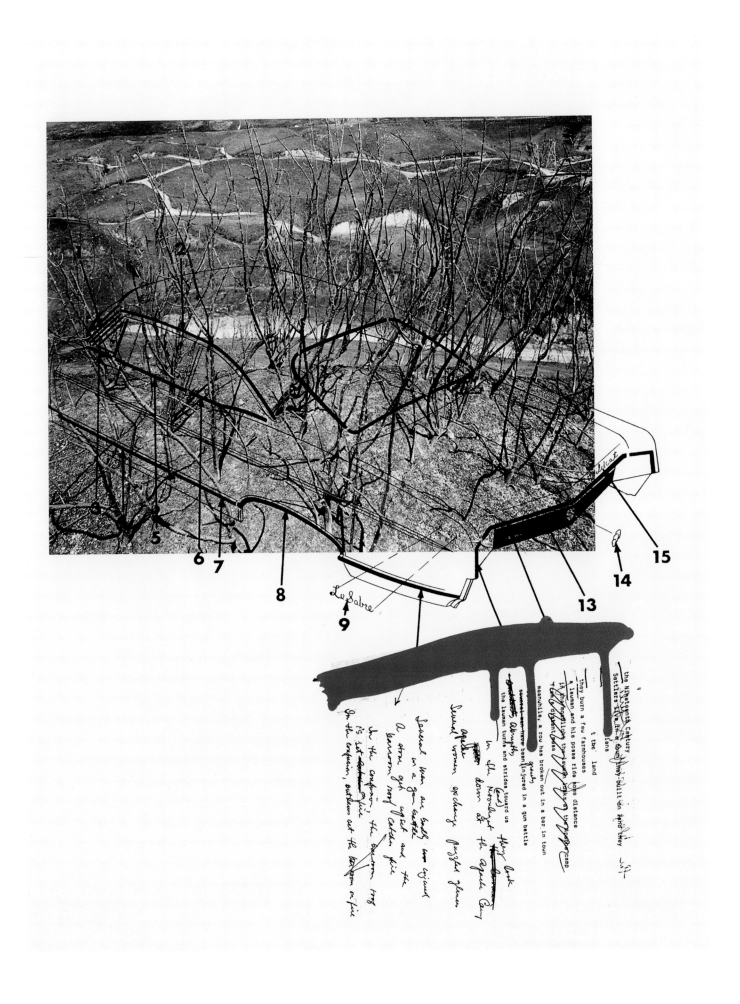

Le Sabre, 1998

Coreopsis, 1998

Untitled (Marble), 1974

Untitled (Fish), 1974

Sidewinder's Delta, 1976

The Contract, 2004

Untitled (Rose Parade), 1966

Rembrandt with Man, 2002

Costume Figures, Amsterdam, 2002

Tiny Draws a Circle, 2003

THE WESTERN EDGE

THE WESTERN EDGE

THE WESTERN EDGE

THE WESTERN EDGE

THE WESTERN EDGE

THE WESTERN EDGE

THE WESTERN EDGE

THE WESTERN EDGE

Foregrounds, 1979

Untitled (Strips), 1974

Untitled (Head/Tail Strips), 1974

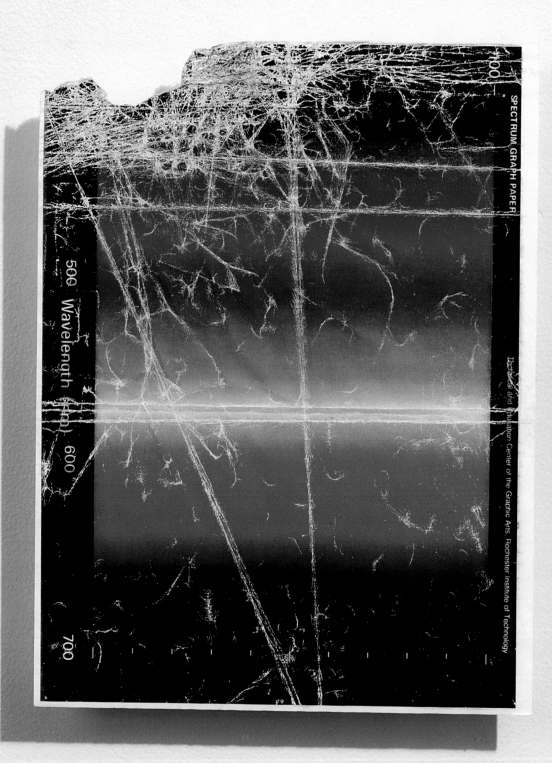

SPECTRUM GRAPH PAPER

Untitled (Spectrum), 1995

Untitled (Camera), 1983
Collection of Gaby and Wilhelm Schuermann, Herzogenrath, Germany

155

Untitled (Torn Portrait), 1980
Collection of Gaby and Wilhelm Schuermann, Herzogenrath, Germany

Untitled (Cathedral), 1980

Untitled (China/Food), 1984

Untitled (Ruled/Scratched), 1975

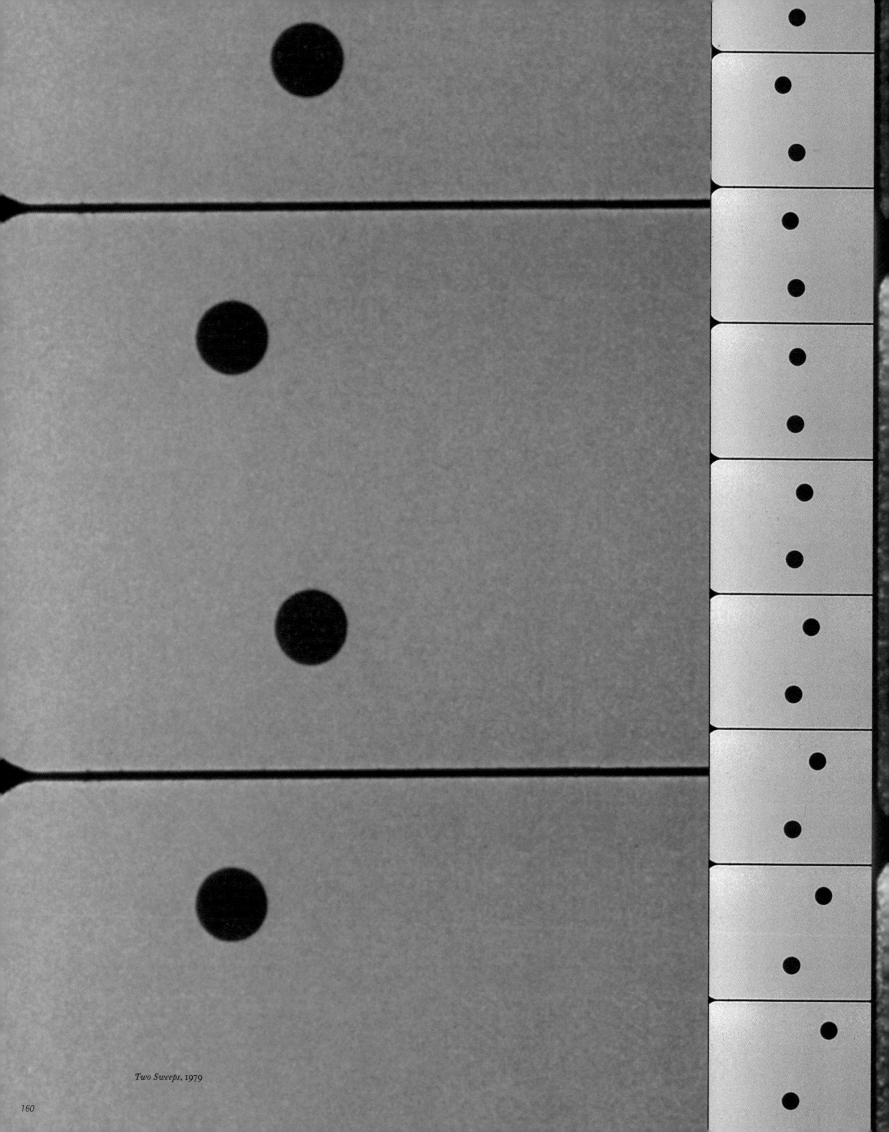

Two Sweeps, 1979

Two Sweeps is a ten-minute loop that presents two images of a circular disc, which is attached to a pendulum. The lateral swing of the pendulum comes to rest in exactly the length of the film, and the two discs operate in opposite direction with regard to time. As one slows, the other accelerates. Both share a common field made of photographic grain; the area within the discs is constant, the surround constantly varies in value. The field around the discs may be seen to be changing in definition, and the question arises as to which is in front of the other.

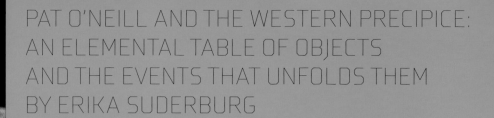

PAT O'NEILL AND THE WESTERN PRECIPICE:
AN ELEMENTAL TABLE OF OBJECTS
AND THE EVENTS THAT UNFOLDS THEM
BY ERIKA SUDERBURG

SOME INTERPRETIVE LANDSCAPES

According to Hopi legend, an ancient race of "Lizard People" dug thirteen underground cities, with a capital located beneath downtown L.A. On January 29, 1934, W. Warren Shufelt, a mining engineer, drilled a 350-foot shaft on North Hill Street looking for the Lizard People. He never found them.[1]

This essay owes its title to Paul Arthur's indispensable essay, "The Western Edge: Oil of L.A. and the Machined Image," *Millennium Film Journal*, no. 12 (1982–83): 8–28.

1. *L.A. Weekly* (January 1996), 17.

Not yet perhaps. But I suggest that Pat O'Neill is on the case and it is only a matter of time before the Lizard People join the O'Neill pantheon of objects, surfaces, luminescences, and topographies in search of celluloid strata. Of course they won't exactly *look* like lizards once they are assimilated. Mr. Shufelt's mistake was depending on a straight line.

This quest for stray items and planes of idiosyncratic but identifiable purpose is a partial key to unlocking O'Neill's filmic production. It is a production best characterized as a steady lava stream of encrusted geologies, interiors, and urban grids—dense and seductive, immersed in western pathos, myth, confusion, and lust. No affixing, pinpointing or sweeping annotation of O'Neill's strata is possible. The artist remains prolific, enigmatic, and passionately engaged in the fabrication and choreography of an eccentric, devastatingly acute visual grammar that defies easy assimilation and seduces the viewer into new perceptual universes.

I'd like to offer the first few pages of a topographical primer to O'Neill's work, an essay slanted geographically and geologically down a Californian desert slope that terminates in either an outlet mall or on a beach. Dorothy Parker said that Los Angeles was seventy-two suburbs in search of a city but this is too-flat East an orientation suggesting only clichéd *vastness* and *lack of weather*. O'Neill's Los Angeles works in seventy-two simultaneous time-space continuums in search of each other. These time warps often sidle into adjacent parking spaces, tease color transparencies, move at sub- or supra-perceptual speeds. His films are rocket-in-time-lapse projectiles that defy linguistic codification and agitate all sensual inputs.

Basically I'd like to make a good sandwich, one that Mr. Schufelt could live off of for a few days down in the mine shaft before Mr. O'Neill unearths him and diverts his linear trajectory.

BEDROCK

To begin, I think I killed O'Neill's goldfish on Lookout Mountain. It should be noted in my defense that this fish swam in dangerous proximity to the optical printer, a contraption of alchemical import and mysterious control switches situated in the middle reaches of mythical Laurel Canyon. Granted, the goldfish was old and not terribly attractive. But I fear I let it languish because I was too immersed in a stack of O'Neill's extra sexy Robert Crumb comics to fully attend to my housesitting rounds. It is upon this fish and the admonishment of a Midwestern film teacher to "go West and *find* Pat O'Neill" that I construct an origin.

I mix this origin in liberally with forbearer smatterings of the roots of graphic cinema, René Clair and Francis Picabia's *Entr'acte* (1924), George Mélies "effects," Viking Eggeling and Hans Richter's collaborations in the 1920s, Walter Ruttman's early *Opus* films (1924–25) and later "documentary" derived "symphonies" of speed and urban mechanics.[2] Folded into this mix would be later-day experimental iconoclasts ranging from Harry Smith's recycling epics to Stan Brakhage's late, hand-painted optical epiphanies and Gene Youngblood's *synaesthetic cinema*.[3] O'Neill represents the friendly collision (possible only in Los Angeles) between myriad elements including abstraction, assemblage, hallucinogens, the sex-education film, Raymond Chandler, Michael Snow remixed by Oskar Fischinger, and a really good 1971 garage band rediscovered and reissued by Rhino Records.

Laurel Canyon and Lookout Mountain Films are the operative fantasy loci— a set of topoi that decidedly inflects all subsequent contributions to this text. From this vantage point, in your peripheral vision a quaalude-diminished Joan Didion careens down Lookout Mountain Avenue in a waxy Lincoln Town Car in search of "senseless killing neighborhoods." The soundtrack is a bootleg jam session between Black Flag and the Art Ensemble of Chicago remixed by Captain Beefheart. It is a Los Angeles of light shows, the experimental film collective, Oasis, secret porno Snow White animation, mosh pits, and a populace that reinvent themselves after ecological disasters. O'Neill is packing up the van with the time-lapse machine and rolling down Lookout Mountain in search of the West and its discontents.[4] He misses sideswiping Joan by a coyote's whisker.

2. Standish Lawder's discussion of Eggeling's quest echos concerns primary to Pat O'Neill's work as well. "Eggeling intended to develop a vocabulary of abstract forms and then to explore its grammar and syntax by combining these forms into 'contrapuntal pairs of opposites', within an all-embracing system based on mutual attraction and repulsion of paired forms." Standish Lawder, *Cubist Cinema* (New York: New York University Press, 1975), 43. Another side in this investigation of abstraction within film language is the rich interface between early cinema and the avant-garde. O'Neill's undisturbed, though accelerated landscapes and their interplay with photographically derived representational objects *and* fabricated multiple graphic interventions is part of this cross-talk between origin cinema and the twenty-first century. For an excellent dissection of early cinema and its influence on the "avant-garde" see Bart Testa, *Back and Forth: Early Cinema and the Avant-Garde* (Toronto: Art Gallery of Ontario, 1992).
3. For an unpacking of graphic cinema and it relationship to European modernism read

Standish Lawder's out-of-print *Cubist Cinema*. Incidentally, as a filmmaker Lawder also resides in the hybridity and optical invention that fuels much of O'Neill's work. In addition, Gene Youngblood's classic *Expanded Cinema* (New York: Dutton, 1970) presages many of the contemporary media arts theoretical parameters and obsessions.
4. In "Distinction of Idioms: Non-Industrial Film in Los Angeles," David E. James puts to rest the cherished binary antagonism theory of experimental production in Los Angeles, the industrial film (Hollywood) grazing in arrogant cannibalism on the "avant-garde" margins (and vice-versa). O'Neill's production supports James's theory of the multi-vocal, the "other dialects of film" present in Los Angeles that complicate the convenient binary. Holly Willis, ed., *Scratching the Belly of the Best: Cutting Edge Media in Los Angeles, 1922–94* (Los Angeles: Filmforum, 1994), 36–37. This catalogue also contains Terry Cannon's overview of the Oasis film collective of which Beverly and Pat O'Neill were co-founding members.

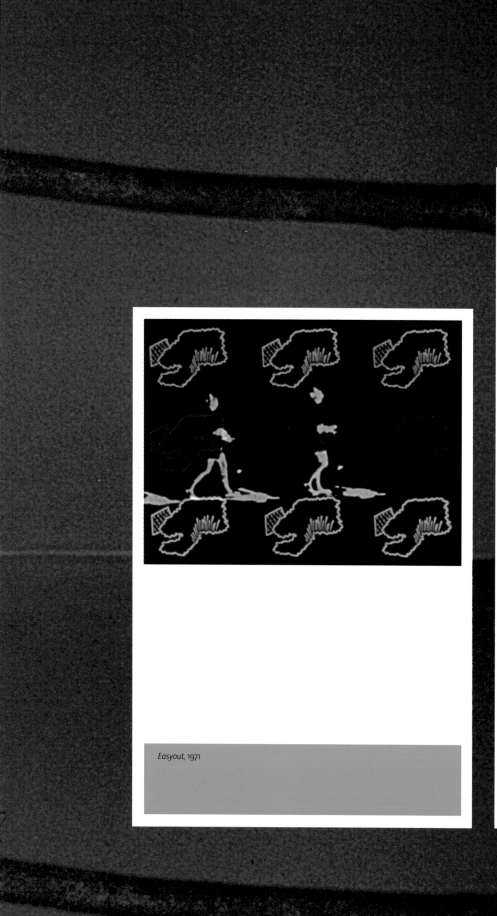

Easyout, 1971

TERMITE, NANOBOT, AND RHIZOMES

Manny Farber writes that, "a peculiar fact about termite-tapeworm-fungus-moss art is that it goes always forward eating its own boundaries, and, likely as not, leaves nothing in its path other than signs of eager, industrious, unkempt activity."[5] As a contrast to what he terms white elephant art—the dead European masterpiece frame as constricting model—termite art "feels its way through the walls of particularization." Termite art is subversive and molecular.

Gilles Delueze and Félix Guattari place what amounts to strategic landmines within Western thought when they posit the existence of the rhizome as the acentered anti-structure: tubers, tunnels, and tangents not necessary emanating from any single origin:

Unlike a structure, which is defined by a set of points and positions, with binary relations between the points and biunivocal relationships between the positions, the rhizome is made only of line: lines of segmentarity and stratification as its dimensions, and the lines of flight or deterritorialization as the maximum dimension after which the multiplicity undergoes metamorphosis, changes in nature. Unlike the tree, the rhizome is not the object of reproduction: nether external reproduction as image-tree not internal reproduction as tree structure. The rhizome is antigeneology. It is short term-memory or anti-memory. The rhizome operates by variation, expansion, conquest, capture, and offshoots. Unlike the graphic arts, drawing, or photography, unlike tracings, the rhizome pertains to a map that must be produced, constructed, a map that is always detachable, connected, reversible, modifiable, and has multiple entryways and exits and its own lines of flight.[6]

O'Neill's films operate by constructing such rhizomes, burrowing into and populating mile-deep strata with shape-shifting nanobots that labor symbiotically with the termite; traveling, occupying, unearthing, and generating.

Section #4 *of Easyout* (1971), laminates multilayers of opaque and transparent color shards and swimming, flickering jagged cells that trigger other planes into synapse color shifts. An overlay grid of growing, hand-drawn corners hovers, attempting to impose order over the flashes of pink, vermilion, green, and yellow cells. The corner edges chew themselves out into transparent complete squares. This gnawed corner grid flicks off when it cannot organize the color flake plane. A slow-motion, yellow silhouette woman saunters across the screen on her independent plane, the grid pops back, morphing into mushroomlike caps that extrude lewd tongues, lapping in her direction. These

5. Manny Farber, "White Elephant Art vs. Termite Art," (1962) in *Movies* (New York: Hillstone Press, 1971), 135.
6. Gilles Deleuze and Félix Guattari, *A Thousand Plateaus: Capitalism and Schizophrenia* (Minneapolis: University of Minnesota Press, 1987), 21.

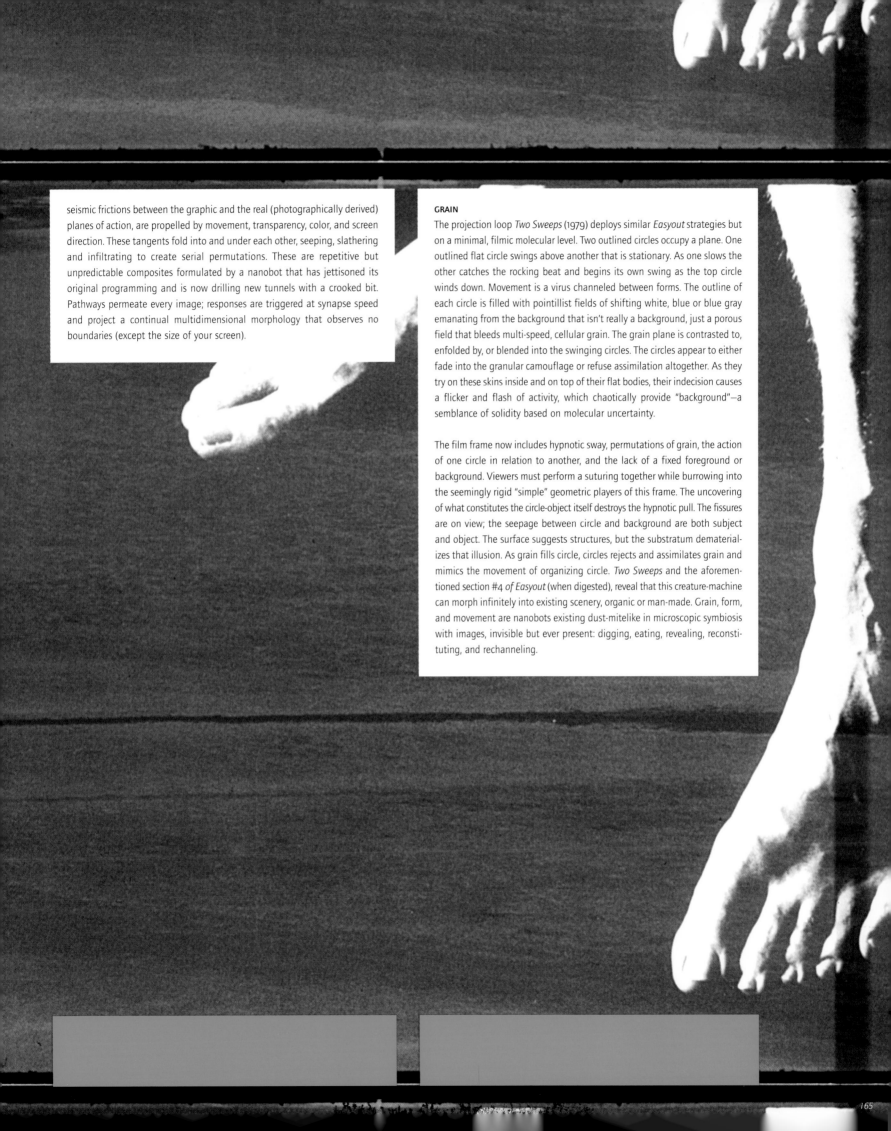

seismic frictions between the graphic and the real (photographically derived) planes of action, are propelled by movement, transparency, color, and screen direction. These tangents fold into and under each other, seeping, slathering and infiltrating to create serial permutations. These are repetitive but unpredictable composites formulated by a nanobot that has jettisoned its original programming and is now drilling new tunnels with a crooked bit. Pathways permeate every image; responses are triggered at synapse speed and project a continual multidimensional morphology that observes no boundaries (except the size of your screen).

GRAIN

The projection loop *Two Sweeps* (1979) deploys similar *Easyout* strategies but on a minimal, filmic molecular level. Two outlined circles occupy a plane. One outlined flat circle swings above another that is stationary. As one slows the other catches the rocking beat and begins its own swing as the top circle winds down. Movement is a virus channeled between forms. The outline of each circle is filled with pointillist fields of shifting white, blue or blue gray emanating from the background that isn't really a background, just a porous field that bleeds multi-speed, cellular grain. The grain plane is contrasted to, enfolded by, or blended into the swinging circles. The circles appear to either fade into the granular camouflage or refuse assimilation altogether. As they try on these skins inside and on top of their flat bodies, their indecision causes a flicker and flash of activity, which chaotically provide "background"—a semblance of solidity based on molecular uncertainty.

The film frame now includes hypnotic sway, permutations of grain, the action of one circle in relation to another, and the lack of a fixed foreground or background. Viewers must perform a suturing together while burrowing into the seemingly rigid "simple" geometric players of this frame. The uncovering of what constitutes the circle-object itself destroys the hypnotic pull. The fissures are on view; the seepage between circle and background are both subject and object. The surface suggests structures, but the substratum dematerializes that illusion. As grain fills circle, circles rejects and assimilates grain and mimics the movement of organizing circle. *Two Sweeps* and the aforementioned section #4 *of Easyout* (when digested), reveal that this creature-machine can morph infinitely into existing scenery, organic or man-made. Grain, form, and movement are nanobots existing dust-mitelike in microscopic symbiosis with images, invisible but ever present: digging, eating, revealing, reconstituting, and rechanneling.

Two Sweeps, 1979

WESTERN

But there is the rhizomatic West... its ever-receding limit, its shifting and displaced frontiers. There is the whole American "map" in the West, where even the trees form rhizomes. America reversed the directions: it put its Orient in the West, as if it were precisely in America that the earth came full circle; its West is the edge of the East. (India is not the intermediary between the Occident and the Orient, as Haudricourt believed: America is the pivot point and mechanism of reversal.) The American singer Patti Smith sings the bible of the American dentist: Don't go for the root, follow the canal...[7]

Paul Arthur writes (in what remains one of the most astute encapsulations of what experimental film "means" within the Los Angeles topography), that "the L.A. area prioritizes a responsiveness to the images and functions of technology and its reflection in past styles of art and mass-cultural production-where 'technology' (in Francis Bacon's original use of the word) means the impulse to culturize the natural, to exert man-made control over materials, processes and their expressive contents."[8] This sense of culturalization is palpable in O'Neill's films and O'Neill himself pinpoints this by saying, "I guess the connection I have with the West is the ground, the earth, and with this sort of human interface between human industry and what was here before we came, which really is about ecological disaster."[9] The western "ground" in O'Neill's frame is open for dissection, breeds new life, and can be dangerous.

A section within *Trouble in the Image* (1996) segments and maps a pine-studded mountain landscape with an ominous, automaton surveillance camera passing over in oiled machine grids. *Water and Power* (1989) is traversed by water pipelines that glint UFOs and dead lakes with underwater urban grids. The re-telling of settler-Indian wars is recounted solely in subtitles over black. An accelerated day and night washes over downtown Los Angeles enclosing a tide of surging and ebbing traffic, glinting and snaking through city corridors accompanied by bugle calls. A sepia Hollywood Moses parts the Red Sea and then cross fades into a sheer face of white quartz. In *Sidewinder's Delta* (1976) a foregrounded giant cactus and lightbulb watch over a solitary stone house with an illuminated blowing curtain window. The bulb and the cactus challenge each other, taking on multiple contrary and then aligned supersaturated colors and then fading out as a generator cut outs on the soundtrack. Simultaneously the lights in the house are extinguished. Cactus and bulb congruently flick into black silhouette as mournful coyotes call. The West as exploitable frontier and promise and the

7. Ibid, 19.
8. Paul Arthur, "The Western Edge," 19.
9. David E. James, "An Interview with Pat O'Neill," *Millennium Film Journal*, nos. 30/31 (Fall 1997): 126.

collapse of that promise coexist awkwardly. O'Neill accesses the landscape through a complex web of objects, textures and sound. The earth, rock, water, and air respond, taking on characters and revealing fields of inquiry and decay. Entropy and shape shifting are the operative movements O'Neill posits as devices to organize, visualize and assimilate the sublime become ordinary and the ordinary become sublime.

Sidewinder's Delta, 1976

The Decay of Fiction, 2002

ALCHEMY

Water and Power provides multiple tracking shots that incorporate objects, drawn landscapes, and the animation of activity incised onto those landscapes. Line-drawn mountain peaks erupt in drawn red flames in the upper background as the foreground tracks, old Western-style storefronts, mammoth wooden dressers with drawers of effluvia, neon signs blinking, stacks of tools, and a geologic strata crossed by speedy time-lapse sunset shadows. Radioactive dot-flame sperm creatures slither out of the hills as time-lapse night engulfs the landscape. Transformation comes through multiple scales, creatures (human or otherwise who activate the space) and entropic slippage. The side of a mountain can be smaller than an overflowing wooden dresser. Tools can be the size of architecture. All objects can potentially transform any other object or site. Alchemy can be inferred and its transformative possibilities manufacture these images. Red can become stone, an incised line can become an ant colony; a glimmer can overtake a lake. Accumulations, manipulation of scale, the breaking down of expectations of the orderly or explainable are the axes of operation. These transmogrifications seem a reasonable response to the Southern California environment.

The Decay of Fiction (2002) modifies this alchemical promise by drifting characters into the decayed shell of the Ambassador Hotel. Although O'Neill constructs a skeleton narrative for *The Decay of Fiction*, his alchemical predilections are intact. A lost woman in a blue dress leads us down a peeling hallway to a door that reveals the bedrock the hotel stands on. Re-occurring interstices—in contradistinction to the flow of ghost figures acting out scenarios within the Ambassador—alternate with characterless shots of architectural landscapes: falling wallpaper like eucalyptus bark, a palm tree shadow climbing the side of a building, blue skies streaking a ballroom wall— in a mind-boggling array of transmutations. The interstices, afloat in a soundstage black void, are bare of any Ambassador architectural referent. These insertions into the "larger" narrative shrink the characters and place them on a tabletop where they mill aimlessly about, while being overseen by a life-sized frenetic time-lapse blurred man, who pages through a book. The pages accelerate until they are on the verge of combustion. It is no accident that floating in these intermediate spaces are objects that smolder and often burst into flame.

FLOW

O'Neill found an envelope labeled "Coreopsis–Helen" with seeds from a 1935 visit his mother had made to her sister in Nebraska. His film *Coreopsis* (1998) was made by scratching into developed and discarded pieces of film stock revealing pink, yellow, and clear layers. This remnant of his memory of her is performed and inscribed in these excised layers. Yellow and pink patterned inscriptions suggest the flower's colors but also recall active photochemical synapses. Scratching notates a kind of hidden liquidity, a harsh inscription, which liberates the constitutive colors hidden in spent stock.

Squirt Gun Step Print (1998) also consists of base materials, raw stock "attacked" with a squirt gun loaded with developer, fixed, and then loop printed. Like *Coreopsis*, *Squirt Gun Step Print* bypasses any camera-recording device. O'Neill's production of these films alongside a work like *The Decay of Fiction* underscores the basic transformative impetus. While Bedrock, film stock, entropic captures, fires, transparent people, and mutating film layers provide an arsenal of perpetual promise in *Coreopsis*, *Squirt Gun Step Print* literally fixes a transformative stream in order to wash the viewer in its macrocosmic projection. Aggregate, translucent, sandwiched, multi-temporal modes of composition require this flow and this definition and return us to what makes film form, what causes film to capture form. Light, color sandwiches, chemical interventions and fixative become the film subject, a subject evocative of memory and a commitment of that memory to non-representational film. Sometimes alchemy is only a squirt gun brandished out the window of a speeding car.

Coreopsis, 1998

SWARMS

In *Trouble in the Image* a twenty-four-second, second segment begins with a full-frame image of the shadows of people waiting for a train in late afternoon sun. The shadows travel from right to left. But a solitary shadow rocks back and forth in the center of the platform. Suddenly temporal space explodes, as the left half of the screen becomes an orange, high-pitched Western U.S. army battle. The soldiers appear to be shooting off screen left and running off screen right directly into the abutted right-hand blue half of the screen. This blue half teems with birds that approximate agitated film grain, moving in swarms according to their own program. The birds engulf a glowing orb that reveals itself (as it is drawn into focus) to be a light bulb on a wire. Overlaying these competing halves is a rotoscoped white line drawing of students writing. A teacher enters and leans in over the student. The teacher straightens up and leans further into the orange frame and appears to witness the original army being overrun by another. The teacher's exit coincides with the blue swarm, which is also exiting the frame in the upper-right-hand corner. An authoritative male announcer describes a light wave experiment involving complementary colors: "yes it's just the spot of red light above, a spot of green light below." The blue and orange complementary halves (already a complex, composited realm) fragment into a quadrant of see-through figures drafted from narrative film engaged in dramatic gestures. Slaps are exchanged and guns pointed. All this has transpired in twenty-four seconds and has involved multiple planes of filmic reality and the suggestions of hundreds more. Perceptually we combine these images and rearrange them depending on which part of the stream we enter. We ascertain and store away for recall as the film continues to accumulate.[10]

Associative memory can lead us to multiple sites: the authority of the education film voice teaching us about light wave travel and color, the pedagogical performance of rotoscoped teacher and learner, the Western movie war providing friction but no climax. The perversity of writing these films destroys the nature of their operation. It is imperative to be in the swarm itself. A viewer returns in warped recall, re-accessing, reinventing and reconfiguring the film. You cannot relate the film using description because O'Neill's films are designed to be inside of them. This interior position (touching down with the swarm), positions the spectator to synaptically link and arrange layers for herself/himself. An O'Neill film will not be perceived nor recalled the same way twice. The impossibility of any visual unity or of a single authorial-based interpretation is clearly present within meticulously constructed composite frames. The hegemony of the maker, the omnipres-ence of his/her apparatus and the radical dissections deployed by O'Neill to control but also open associative meaning make entering his work at once tantalizing and multi-sensory. Art historical, filmological descriptions can not illuminate the density of O'Neill's project for such accounts necessarily suggest organizational linearity, but the fecund tubers of a rhizome (of which this essay is one tentative subterranean tendril) breaking off and sprouting new linkages in a twenty-four-second crackle begin perhaps to articulate why dwelling in O'Neill's substrata is so deeply pleasurable.

10. For a close analysis of O'Neill's practice see the meticulous articles of Christine Noll Brinckmann and Grahame Weinbren, "The O'Neill Landscape: Four Scenes From Foregrounds," *Millennium Film Journal*, nos. 4/5 (Summer/Fall 1979): 101–16 and "Selective Transparencies: Pat O'Neill's Recent Films," *Millennium Film Journal*, no. 6 (Spring 1980): 51–72.

CRUST

It rested on a crust of earth at the edge of a sea that ended a world.[11]

What I mean by this allegorical tension is precisely that there is this space of reading, of losing, of delaying, of thinking, that is folded right into a gap and stop -gap of recent history. That isn't a place of metaphorical or metaphysical comforts, of big histories, of ancient histories, but instead Los Angeles opens onto recent history in a catastrophic and primal way. Adorno said that it is always recent history that flashes back as primal. It's only recent history under mega-history that comes up for allegorical reflection over and over again in L.A., in ways finely suited to its being in the center field of all kinds of mediatic representations. Here the gap, the psychologized, mobilized preparedness is slightly differently skewed and framed but finally also caught up in a recent history of forgetting, of sudden remembering, of lapses and flashbacks, of all those discontinuities that I first ran into when I thought I would walk around L.A. for the first time.[12]

O'Neill's primal scene includes tar pits, freeway flow, the educational film, and the grain of technologically aided human paranoid construction. In the later third of *Sidewinder's Delta* a brick brandished by an off-screen mechanism creakily careens from one side of the screen to the other like a wrecking ball. Its scale dwarfs the translucent building on the side of a desert highway. It is circling and slowly builds up speed. The building is one of those quickie slab structures of indeterminate use. The wall facing forward translucently leaks the landscape of a ribbon highway backed by mountains. This wall is transparent but maintains structural integrity. The brick creaks heavily and circles closer. Gunshots are heard, and the screen goes black before the moment of immanent destruction. Closure is denied, but inference continues to reverberate. We don't see the correct images paired to the aural landscape. Our expectations are disrupted, and O'Neill happily lays plastic explosives in the gaps of narrative illusion.

You have to have a sense of humor about the end of the world, particularly because the world is always ending here in California. We are an edge cult, a clichéd and sometimes very real designation. Scrapping around that crusty edge and forming new mud shapes staves off the end for a bit. The West that O'Neill traverses is alternately fated and closed but nonetheless resonant with strange promises and perpetually reinvented finalities. Today clear-cutting and organic farming co-exist in a California governed by a robotoid action figure. It is this schizophrenic identity that O'Neill uncovers and explores. He

deploys co-existing stratas of obsolescence, repose, revolution, consumption, and anarchic agitation. Ultimately he engages us in seeing. As he puts it "we are shoppers in the second-hand store of technology adapting illusion machines to remind one another of the simplicity of experience itself."[13]

Now, that's a sandwich I'd send my nanobot out for.

11. Frank Fenton from his novel *A Place in the Sun* quoted in Carey McWilliams, *Southern California: An Island on the Land* (Salt Lake City: Peregrine Smith Books, 1946, 1973), 269. There is no understanding of Southern California without Carey McWilliams.
12. Author's video interview with Laurence A. Rickels, author of *The Case of California*, (Baltimore and London: Johns Hopkins University Press, 1991).

13. Pat O'Neill, *The Journal of Film and Video* 54, no. 1 (Spring 2002).

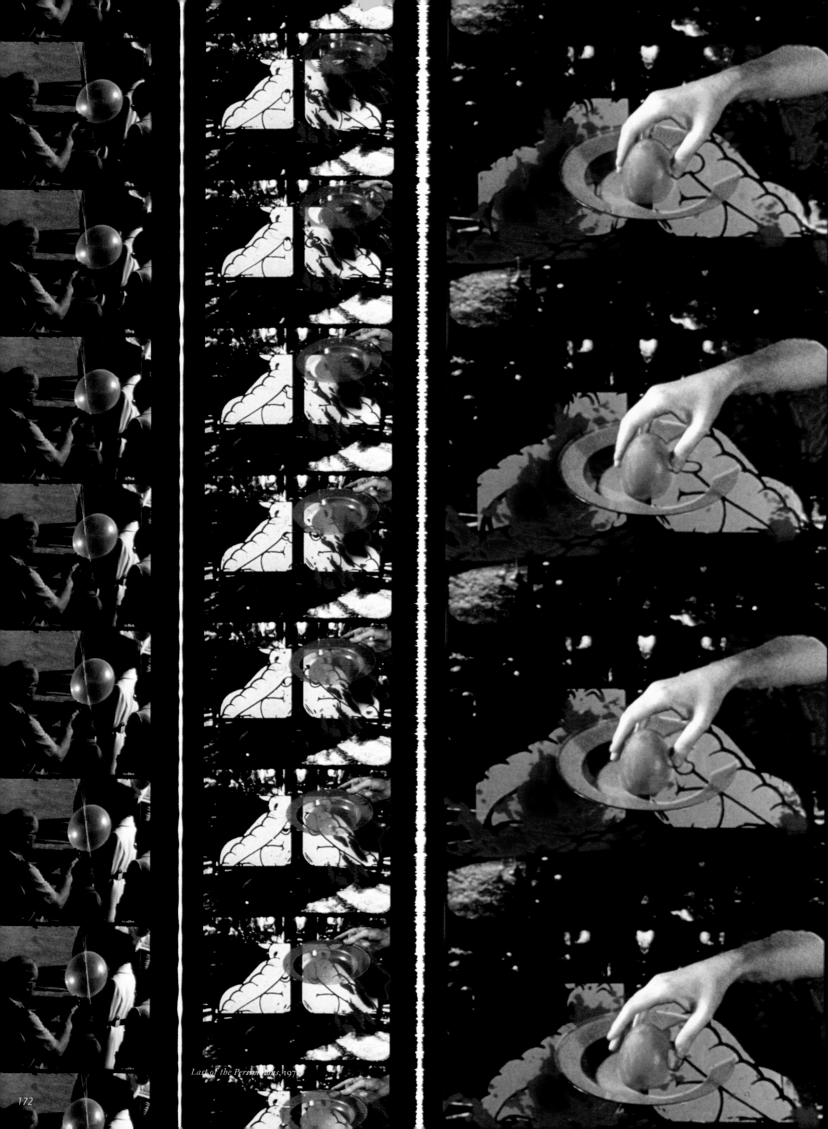

Last of the Persimmons, 1973

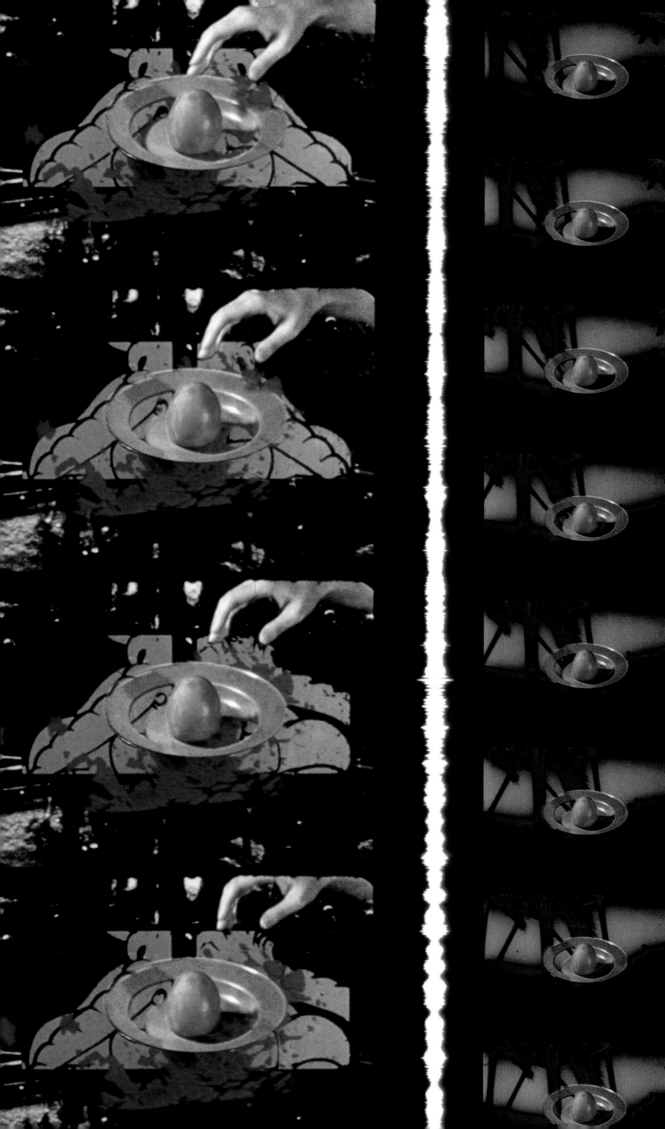
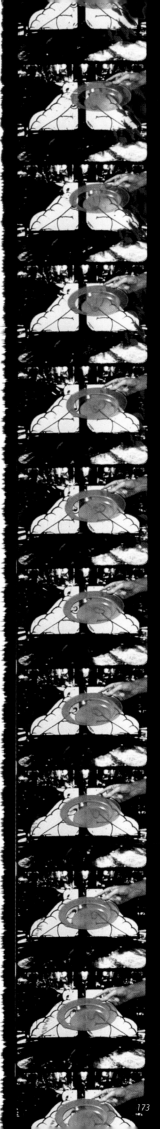

Fat Tree, 1999
Collection of Gaby and Wilhelm Schuermann, Herzogenrath, Germany

During Fall Too Blue, 1990

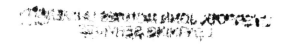

Seated Coil, 1985

Final Island, 2003

Bar Wall, Ajo, 1992

Two Figures with Water Tower, 1997

Bamboo Action Map, 2003

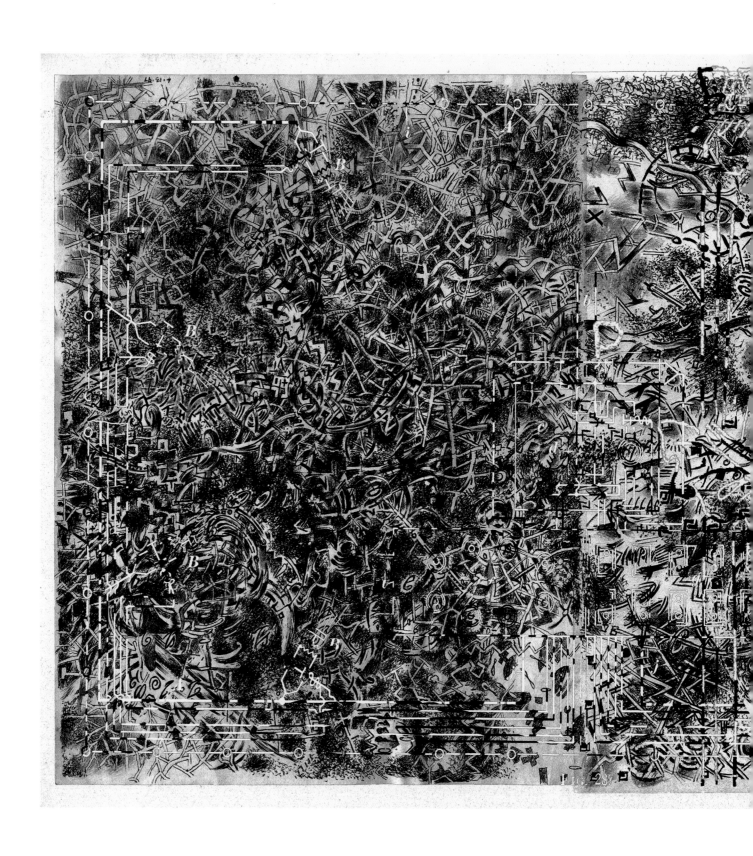

Carpet 1, 2003

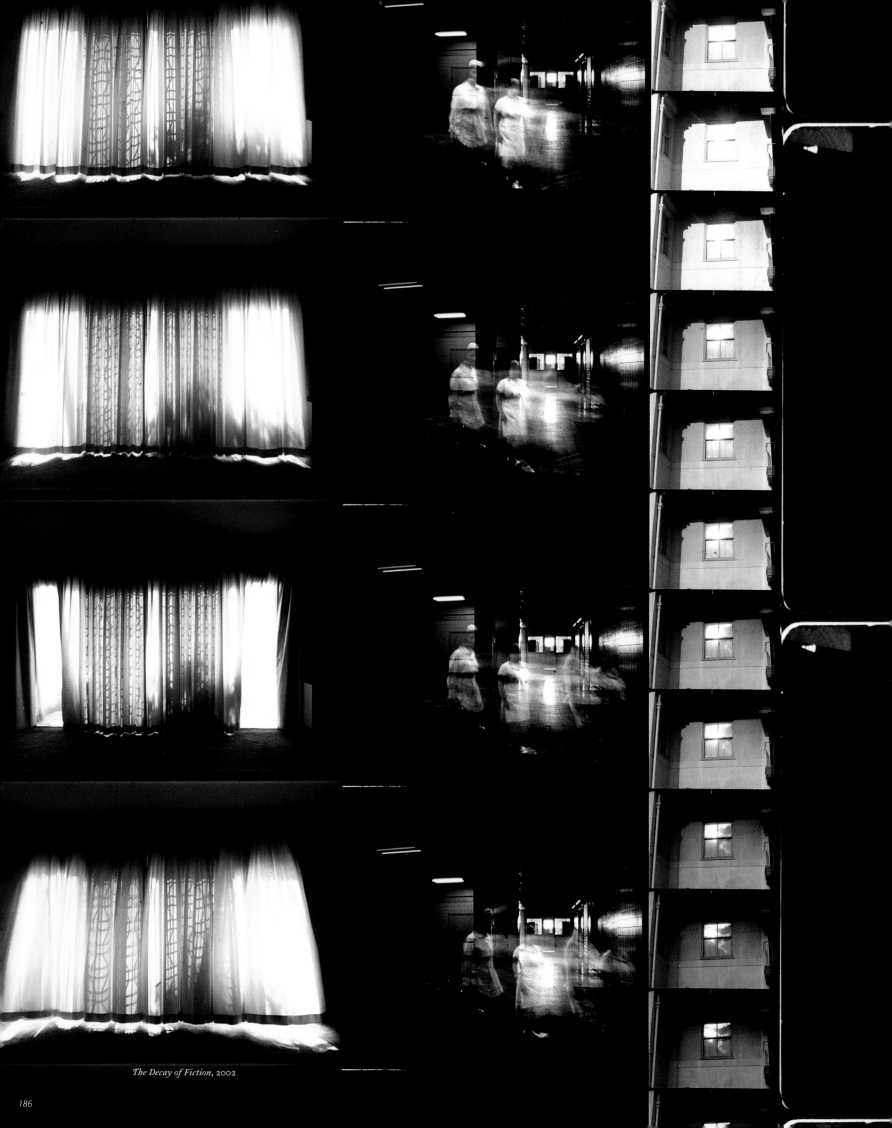

The Decay of Fiction, 2002

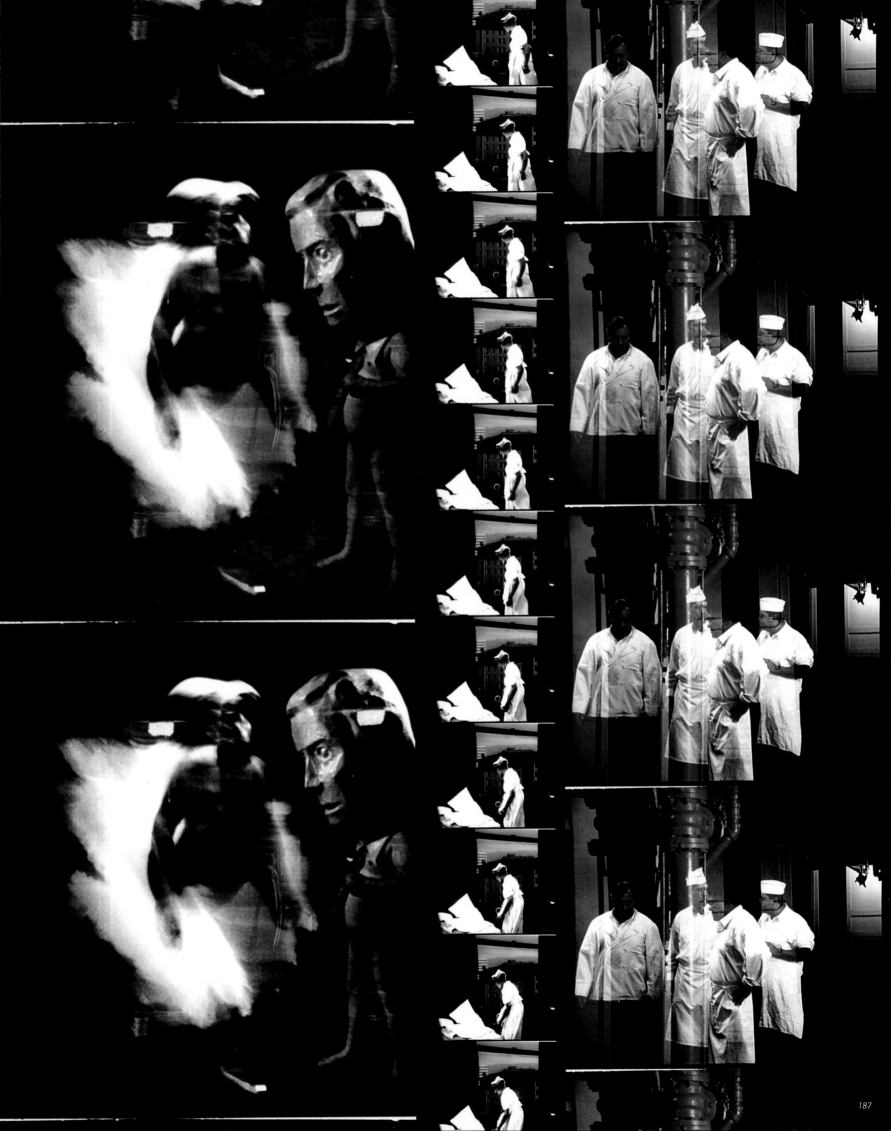

LEFT: *Untitled (Phone Boxes)*, 1993
RIGHT: *Untitled (detail, South Patio)*, 1993

Untitled (Overhead View of South Patio), 1993

Tracing The Decay of Fiction: Encounters with a Film by
Pat O'Neill, 2002 (Installation view)

Tracing The Decay of Fiction: Encounters with a Film by Pat O'Neill, 2002 (Installation view)

The Decay of Fiction, 2002

A CONVERSATION WITH PAT O'NEILL

In early December 2003, I spent two days in conversation with Pat O'Neill at his new home in Pasadena, California, which he shares with his wife Beverly. Pat and Beverly are key figures in the Southern California art world. For over forty years, Pat has been a leading independent filmmaker and has contributed to the film culture of Los Angeles, both as an artist and as an organizer of experimental film screenings. With a group of artists and filmmakers, Pat and Beverly founded the Los Angeles film cooperative Oasis in 1976 fostering local support for and knowledge of alternative films. For many years Beverly also served as Provost at the California Institute of the Arts (CalArts), an institution with a major film school and animation program.

I have always been fascinated by Southern California, and Pat's films embody its many contradictions. Although I included *Water and Power* in the 1991 Whitney Museum of American Art Biennial and had followed Pat's filmmaking for many years, I did not know him like I did other Southern California film and video artists, such as Morgan Fisher and Bill Viola. So I welcomed the opportunity to interview Pat for the catalogue of this timely and important exhibition. In preparation for our meeting, I immersed myself in Pat's films, seeing many of them again, and I spent time looking at his digital photographs and reading through the notebooks he provided me. While Pat's films have been honored nationally and internationally, they are long overdue for focused critical attention. Through our conversation I came to know Pat better and gained a greater understanding of his work. And I was continually impressed by the modesty of his observations as he candidly reflected on his creative life. I believe Pat is one of the foremost artists of our time, and my conversation with him reinforced that opinion.

Many of Pat's films are uncanny meditations on place and history. He has approached filmmaking as a bricoleur, shaping seamless moving-images that echo the narratives, myths, and stories embedded in the everyday culture of Los Angeles and its suburban and rural surroundings. Oscillating between past and present, mythic and mundane, his art conveys a sense of melancholy that captures the chimerical seductions of Southern California and the Western landscape. Although Pat has always worked with complete independence, his films possess a sophisticated understanding of Hollywood. While retaining a solid distance between his art and the all-consuming power of popular culture, he has fashioned an artistic identity and creative life that includes collecting film footage fragments from such sources as cartoons, newsreels, and Hollywood movies.

In recent years museums have steadily integrated the moving-image artwork into exhibition programs and collections, just as galleries have increasingly realized the commercial potential of moving-image installations and projections. The various forms of the moving image have impacted all of the arts. Museums and galleries must now address the urgent need of preserving this body of work. In tandem with preservation, art historians and curators face the challenge of rethinking twentieth-century art history so as to place film, video, and new media alongside the other arts. Pat O'Neill's films occupy an important but as yet largely unanalyzed place in this history. He expanded the vocabulary of filmmaking and instituted an editing style that is not unlike that of a jazz musician who creates music in time with the contemporary tempo. And like a jazz composer, Pat has forged an urban art form. He is an individual voice alternately speaking for a community or listening into the ever-changing migratory rhythms of the highways and railroads. As complex documents of the cultural fabric, Pat's films articulate abstract and representational images, and explore the light, color, and texture of movements in time.

John G. Hanhardt

Q: John G. Hanhardt
A: Pat O'Neill

Q: I thought we might begin with your most recent film, *The Decay of Fiction* [2002]. For me, it is about memory and place. With those themes in mind, I would like to ask you about how you first came to film. What was it that drew you to it? When did your interest in it emerge? And what informed that beginning?

A: I began thinking about film around 1961, when I was a graduate student in Fine Arts at UCLA. I was coming from an undergraduate design program, also at UCLA, during which I had increasingly concentrated on photography. I began making serial projections of transparencies, followed by loop projections in 16mm film, and finally short films. It was an extension of studio practice, using the film camera and projector in conventional and unconventional ways to make and present images over time. Everything was open to consideration—projection on objects, on performers, on materials of varying opacity, and inside sculptural containers.

Q: Where did you grow up?

A: In south Los Angeles, right on the border of Inglewood, in a working-class and middle-class neighborhood that is essentially a flat grid. I went to UCLA and moved into a trailer near the Venice canals.

Q: What were your interests growing up?

A: Automobiles fascinated me early on. I was always an avid model builder, and, between the age of fourteen and seventeen, I constructed entries for the Fisher Body Craftsmen's Guild, a national contest for teenage boys sponsored by General Motors. Contestants built scale-model prototype cars. Each model required months of shaping clay, carving balsa wood, turning metal parts, and spray-painting lacquer surfaces. I never knew another person who entered.

1938 Chevrolet, Los Angeles, 1957   FBCG model, 1957   1959 Ford powered roadster, 1964

Q: What brought you to UCLA and what was your experience there?

A: By the end of high school I was intent on a career as a designer of cars. I was accepted at UCLA, which was virtually tuition free. The design program at UCLA, part of the art department, was in an ascendant period. The program's founder, Henry Dreyfuss, had framed industrial design as a socially conscious discipline bridging engineering, ergonomics, and esthetics. Studying design yielded a foundation in problem solving and communication with far-reaching benefits for me. Those years exposed me to art for the first time, not only in art history classes but also through contact with practicing painters and sculptors. The autonomy of the artist, or at least the fantasy of autonomy, struck me as different from the life of a designer.

By my fourth year at UCLA I had decided to do my graduate studies in the fine arts. Not that I had any affinity with the esthetics of my art teachers. Quite the contrary, I was aware of the first manifestations of Pop Art and Fluxus and had spent hours in the library learning all I could about Surrealism, a history rarely touched upon in the curriculum and pejoratively dismissed by studio instructors. They applauded genteel figurative and abstract work. I hungered to be a part of what I perceived as a revolution in the concept of artistic practice.

One of my instructors in graphic design was Robert Heinecken, whose trajectory was similar to my own. He was a designer who came to embrace photography. He undertook the radical project of liberating photography from mechanical technique and sought to establish it as an art form in its own right. This was a battle that had been going on for at least a century but had not yet touched the fine arts department at UCLA. His success in this struggle originated a new course of study.

I found the discussions in Heinecken's classes to be particularly relevant to real-life questions. I was captivated by the idea of the photographic image as a mirror of the maker's mind and a revelation of belief, instinct, and heritage.

I became Heinecken's second graduate student. He was a maverick in that he welcomed transgressions of the purity of the medium. We were encouraged to distort the technology, cook the negative, cut up the print, and even use its surface to paint upon.

About this time I became aware of the Coronet, a theater on La Cienega Boulevard that showed a repertory of unusual films: works by the 1920s European avant-garde, Kenneth Anger, Maya Deren, Buñuel and Dalí's *Andalusian Dog*, and Bruce Conner's *A Movie*. Raymond Rohauer operated the theater and Stan Brakhage worked there for a while as a projectionist.

Q: So during your undergraduate years you gradually moved away from design to focus on photography. And your interest in photography led you to film. Aside from Heinecken, were there other teachers who mentored you or were important to you?

A: Bob Heinecken was my principal advisor, but there were at least two others who were important to me. One was Donald Chipperfield. He had been Heinecken's teacher as well. Chipperfield had a reputation as a taskmaster, but those who stayed with his teaching were often grateful for the level of concentration they learned to tap into. His photo critiques tended to uncover life-changing levels of awareness. Another person was John Neuhart, a design instructor who was also a graphic and exhibition designer in the office of Charles and Ray Eames. Neuhart's approach reflected the practice of the Eamses; he maintained openness to and engagement with every aspect of world culture and its visual manifestations. He possessed an encyclopedic knowledge of image-making and image-reproduction techniques. By comparison, the fine arts faculty seemed antiquated and phobic about popular culture and non-traditional media. As Neuhart's assistant I taught the use of the letterpress and ran the silkscreen lab.

Film editing,
UCLA Art Department, 1962

Robert Abel, 1963

Film editing, UCLA Art Department, 1962

Film drying rack, 1962

Q: Let's talk about your photographic work, which began around 1960 at UCLA. You mentioned your renewed interest in working with the still image. Could you expand on what distinguishes your still work from your film work? I would say from the outset that the still images contain distinctive features that also define your work as a film artist.
A: I started by making stills on the optical printer. I would select a frame that seemed to stand for the work and send it out to be printed somewhere. In the early 1980s, I got interested in making unique frames that were not part of films. These compositions were more compressed and more interesting as a single image.

I got to thinking about the viewer's experience of the static image. It is not just experienced as a whole. You also explore it. Usually there's an instinctive place to enter the composition and then move through it, experiencing the space. You begin to know the imagery and figure out what the tensions are in it.

Some of the same imagery appears in both my films and my still images. For instance, I have used the form of the coil a lot. It appears in the still image *Seated Coil* and in the film *Trouble in the Image*. It contains energy and functions as a focal point. In the still image I superimposed the coil on a background that's made up of part of a ruin and a landscape of burning chaparral. When the negative came back I decided to put a couple of humanlike legs on the coil. I scratched the legs into the emulsion with a point, and then printed from that.

Q: What changed when you began to work digitally?
A: Once digital inkjet printing became available in the 1990s I was able to make really good quality prints. By the mid-1990s I was working with a couple of commercial printers, making images of some size. In 1997, I bought a computer and things really began to expand. Now I can scan my whole library of images, commercial graphics, and found bits of paint. I can arrange them in digital files

and try them with one another. With this great facility, the visual problems get to be really interesting. At first I was bothered by the fact that I was working on a platform that was not of my own invention. I worried it would be invasive. But then I realized I could work with complete freedom with the photographs and materials I was familiar with. It was revolutionary. Some people have said, "well, anybody can do that." Well perhaps anybody can, but on the other hand, the English language is the same way, anybody can write it, but only a few people can write it well and they're still the same words.

Q: Do you see a relationship between your use of the optical printer and the still images you are making?
A: Yes, the principles are the same but the experience is fluid. I can speculate much more. With the optical printer you can never see the whole thing until you have brought all the pieces together and put them into film format, made an exposure test for each one, and then tried them. It's a long process. Working digitally everything is up for grabs all the time.

Q: Was film part of your classroom experience or was your primary exposure at the Coronet?
A: In the film school, Hugh Gray's classes in Russian revolutionary cinema and the European avant-garde were extremely popular. Through Gray I encountered Dziga Vertov, Eisenstein, Ruttman, Rene Clair, and Slavko Vorkapich. He invited Josef Von Sternberg to class. I also met Beverly Morris there, and we've been married for forty years.

Among my classmates, Peter Mays, a painter who was just getting into filmmaking, established a film society at UCLA, inviting filmmakers to screenings. Two of the first to come were Jack Smith and Gregory Markopolous. Markopolous had a paper bag full of camera rolls, which he screened. They became part of

Studio (detail), Santa Monica, 1967   Studio (detail), Santa Monica, 1967   Studio window with untitled sculpture, Santa Monica, 1967

Twice a Man. Stan Brakhage screened *Dog Star Man*, part one, and spoke at length. That film did not engage me at the time, but I found him fascinating.

Soon I began attending "Movies Around Midnight," a screening series of "underground" films presented by John Fles on Saturday nights at the Cinema Theater on Western Avenue in Hollywood. It was at these late-night screenings that I encountered the first of the Warhol films. I also saw works by the Kuchar Brothers, Ron Rice, Carolee Schneeman, the Newsreel group from Berkeley, Jordan Belson, Brakhage, and the touring program of the Ann Arbor Film Festival. The screenings began as small events. Within a few months, the Cinema Theater, which had about 400 seats, was full to overflowing, initiating another screening on Friday nights. But it only lasted a few years and was definitely over by 1965.

Q: And in 1963 you made your first film, *By the Sea*. What led to that first film?

A: Well, I had been gravitating toward Venice since high school. Venice was a beach town stuck in time. Abbott Kinney began developing it in 1903 as a residential and resort community. It had a system of canals, crossed by elegant concrete bridges. There was an amusement pier with a ballroom. But Venice failed as a residential development, and the 1920 oil boom radically changed the face of the waterfront. Vacant lots became well sites. By the late 1950s, most of the wells were played out, but their wooden and steel derricks still stood. The region was melancholy, particularly in winter, with the scent of the ocean mixing with crude oil and dead things—floating in the canal—a slum by the sea. Rents were cheap and one could still find storefront studio space. San Francisco's Beat culture put in a brief Southern California appearance there. My apprenticeship in photography took place in Venice, in the no-man's land of derricks, tanks, empty houses, and oil-slicked canals. It was unfamiliar, largely vacant, and fraught with expressive possibility.

Just a few miles north was the Santa Monica Pier, with its ancient carousel, carnival games, and corn-dog stands. Nearby was Muscle Beach, a hangout for bodybuilders, circus performers, and precocious teenage gymnasts. There was always some action to watch and an enthusiastic audience. No one seemed to object to the presence of a camera, even the whirring Bolex, which I had borrowed from my friend Bob Abel. As footage accumulated we started to think about how it could be put together. Bob got access to a film school editing room with an upright Moviola editor, and we began to cut. At around the same time, I was printing photos on a graphic arts sheet film that produced very interesting results—a long tonal range with very dense blacks. I enlarged sequences shot at the beach with the Bolex, controlling the exposure so that the ground completely disappeared, leaving figures to float in a void. Bob and I experimented with making this happen in motion. It seemed like a way to transform flexing, stretching, and flying bodies into creatures that had never before been seen on the screen. This material was the basis of *By the Sea*. It was my only collaboration with Bob, who later became well known as an innovative producer of visual graphics for television commercials.

Q: What about the transition from *By the Sea* to *7362*, which is from 1967? In the history of video, this is the moment that Paik developed the image processor. At the same time, you, using an optical printer, were making *7362*, which is exceptionally rich visually. Can you talk about the transition from *By the Sea* to *7362* in terms of abstraction, color, and the processing of the image?

A: In 1966 I was teaching photography at UCLA, standing in for Heinecken during a sabbatical year. As a state employee I had access to an institution that sold surplus materials from various government agencies. They had contact printers that had been used by the Navy for combat film work. I bought a contact

British Columbia Sweep, 1968   *Large Sweep #2*, 1969   *Black Mountain Sweep*, 1967   *Safer Than Springtime*, 1966

printer and put it in one of the UCLA darkrooms. It was a Bell & Howell, Model J, a beautiful machine that was long out of production. It allowed me to print one-to-one from any negative to any stock. I also obtained processing tanks so I could hand-develop black-and-white stock. This led to the possibility of doing various photographic processes, like the Sabatier effect, or solarization. I was interested in making something that was neither a negative nor a positive, but an amalgam of both. The technique emphasizes outlines of shapes and the boundaries between them but largely obscures their surfaces. The contact printer gave me the possibility of taking a piece of film and reproducing it many times. I could take a single figure and make a chorus line.

At this point I had completely left design except as an occasional source of income. In addition to photography and film, I was tentatively beginning to realize some ideas in sculpture. The early pieces were constructions of appliance parts, military gear, and industrial scrap metal. I started lighting and filming some of these same materials, often on turntables or pendulums. This led to constructing a stage apparatus, in which to record live models performing machinelike movements. This footage could be combined on the contact printer to yield hybrids of the living and inanimate. One day I tried printing the same piece of negative twice on the same raw stock, turning it over between exposures. This produced a bilateral symmetry in which every movement was fused with its opposite. This technique became the primary structural motive of *7362*.

Q: So something important synthesized around *7362*. Bilateral splitting is an image-processing technique. But you were also interested in the philosophic and materialist notion of the object, which is complicated by this process of doubling. I am fascinated by the connections you have suggested between image processing, sculpture, and film. Through processing you seem to have imbued film with tactility.

A: *7362* had to do with hand-making, with being able to take something, do an operation on it, look at it, do another operation, and so on. It was a mechanical model, predating the electronic. My interaction was with film and light. *7362* is the Kodak stock number of a high contrast black-and-white film that is used in the making of film titles and mattes. That stock was the basic material for many of the intermediate steps in the film's making. It was the missing link Abel and I didn't know about when we made *By the Sea*.

Q: The film *Screen*, from 1969, explores the celluloid grain. Can you talk about this technique and how it developed?

A: Initially I used spray paint on clear film. I would spray a section of film and then make several different versions on high-contrast black-and-white film. These were printed on color-reversal film using theater lighting gels to produce color. *Screen* was the first film I made on an optical printer. I made it for a group show, in January 1969, called "Electric Art" that was curated by the sculptor Oliver Andrews.

Q: Did you think of *Screen* as sculpture?

A: No, I thought of it as a non-photographic image that was projected continuously as a loop. The projector was concealed in a booth. One of the walls of the booth had a perfectly square opening—I think it was four feet by four feet—fitted with a back projection screen. Being square helped to remove the work from the definition of a movie. The film appeared to be built into the wall's surface.

Q: Your film *Runs Good*, from 1970, is a brilliant mix of found footage—from science education, newsreel, and stag films, to blocks of monochromatic color. And the sound quality is also distinctive. Compared to the films we've discussed so far, *Runs Good* captures and remixes a whole other set of source images.

Santa Cruz, 1965   Santa Cruz, 1966   Beverly and Pat O'Neill, Colorado, 1966

A: Before *Runs Good* I did another film, called *Bump City* [1964]. It's the first work in which I deal with a vision of urbanity, a vision of an environment driven by commerce. That film used neon signs, animated billboards, and print-ads for cigarettes to construct a whimsically hellish vision of a mediated society. That film led me to begin collecting castoff films. Although I didn't actually use any stock footage in *Bump City*, when I got to *Runs Good*, I had amassed several hours of film sequences that I had copied on the contact printer. I also consulted the Los Angeles Central Public Library, which had a 16mm collection that could be borrowed by teachers. And there was a wonderful little business in the San Fernando Valley called Gaines Films that dealt in 16mm prints. I bought newsreel stuff, Castle Films releases, television shows—such as "You Asked For It," "Beverly Hillbillies," Alfred Hitchcock, and "Twilight Zone"—and industrial sales and training films there. The Gainses also sold footage by the pound. You might get lucky, or you might get a whole lot of leader. Another good source of discarded film was sound fill, which was sold for use as leader. These sources were a reward for staying in Hollywood.

Q: Isn't "runs good," a term used for a car? As in, "used car, runs good?"
A: Yes. It's a very minimal claim and you still see it on windshields. *Runs Good* is deeply ironic. This was 1970. You can see a reaction to a society that seemed to be on the edge of self-destruction. It has many parallels with Conner's *A Movie*, made twelve years earlier.

Q: Tell me about your use of monochromatic color in this film. For me, it raises the issue of postmodernism. You take narrative material but move past it by acknowledging modernist frames of reference.
A: When I was working on *Runs Good* I visited the Berkeley Art Museum and looked at the Hans Hofmann canvasses in its collection. I was familiar with

Clement Greenberg's writings and Hofmann's writings on color. I was thinking about the idea of optical recession and advance, how colors occupy space depending on hue, saturation, and contrast with the field. So in *Runs Good* I made two windows—just like holes through the screen—which allowed for two colors to interact and gradually change independent from the black-and-white background. The images I chose as background were all news shots that had central characters in them, so that they would be situated in the middle of the screen between the two windows. I found a roll of film of someone being booked into jail and covering his face. When I hid part of the image, the conflict was very immediate. There are two realities going on, and you can attend to both of them at the same time but only by using different parts of your mind. One part is engaged with absorbing a reportorial image of a personality, a straightforward recording of something that undoubtedly was shown with a voiceover. The other part is experiencing the interactions of color.

Q: I was really taken by *Easyout*, from 1971. You collaborated with Stan Levine on the sound, which I thought was very interesting. Also your use of loops struck me as something that a new generation of artists would benefit from seeing.
A: The looped section is taken from Max Fleischer's *Betty Boop* cartoons from the 1930s and early 1940s. They were just old enough that my generation hadn't experienced them as kids. And they had a very bold, very strong line that I could reproduce over and over again. By this time, I had done a lot of work with Marty Muller, an extraordinary painter and brilliant cartoonist who was my creative collaborator, along with his lady-friend and later wife [filmmaker and painter], Chick Strand. As a painter he went by the name Neon Park. In some ways his humor reminds me of the German artist Michael Sowa. We worked for several years with vintage cartoons, cycling motions over and over, and sometimes

Beverly O'Neill, Santa Cruz, 1966   Carl Cheng, New York, 1966   Pat O'Neill, New York, 1966

redirecting the stories into peculiar conclusions. I tried to make a field of motions so completely assimilated that you were not aware of the individual parts. We took things—like rolling rocks going down a hill, splashing water, or elephants dancing—and printed them over and over until they moved like primordial rubble. Yet it still had the eight-frame rhythmical beat of Fleisher's animation.

Q: At this point you began bringing found footage into your filmmaking. This calls to mind the work of Wallace Berman and his interest in assemblage and collage. Were you aware of Berman's work at this time?

A: Wally Berman did posters for "Movies Around Midnight." He lived in Beverly Glen, where I lived during my graduate school days. Wally had a studio near the market. He would often hang out at the market, chatting with neighbors and digging through the trash. I did not know who he was at the time, although I had seen his famously shutdown show through the window at the Ferus Gallery.

For me, existing images were a natural place to begin. I was always trying to make an image that could not be preconceived. At the same time I wanted to have a starting point that was somehow socially defined. It always had to do with creating interconnections, ending up with something that went beyond its parts.

Q: There is a rich iconography of found and generated footage in *Last of the Persimmons* [1972]. Can you speak about how the imagery in this work came about?

A: It started out very simply. It was a celebration of a place where there were three persimmon trees. Every fall we'd be up to our navels in sweet sticky fruit. Most people did not know that you are supposed to wait to eat them until they are really ripe. They are very bitter when they are still hard. So I made this little training film. It starts in the aftermath of a Pasadena Rose Parade. A man is

blowing up balloons and people are looking at the flower-covered floats. Crowds of strolling citizens are examining elaborate temporal art pieces. Everyone seems contented, because the art is clearly labeled and thematically determined. Then a green plate appears with a red fruit on it. You see hands preparing the fruit. In the background is a pattern of repeated linear animations, like wallpaper. The animations replace the tabletop, making the dish appear to float.

Q: *Down Wind* [1973] has time-lapses. Had you used them before?

A: No, I started shooting time-lapses in 1972. *Down Wind* began as a diary of a year that included some travel in Europe. The organizing principle of *Down Wind* is the diagonally moving plane that cuts through the shots. This plane is different from the rest of the imagery and draws a distinction between the screen's surface and the illusions projected on it. Of course, it is an illusion as well. The shots document the consumption of the unfamiliar as a summertime diversion—a cat show, geysers, a dance of two gloved hands, a clock made out of flowers in Switzerland. But the film is really about the experience of looking at a screen, it gives the screen itself a character independent from the movie.

Q: So on a micro level the animation frame anticipates some of the compositional ideas behind *Saugus Series* [1974]?

A: At the time I was still editing in a cinematic way, searching for ways to cut on action, to propel the experience as smoothly as possible, and to use sound as an agent in transitions. *Saugus Series* is segmented. Around 1973 I became frustrated with my editing assumptions. In *Saugus* I wanted to make shots with a fixed number of elements that would be present from beginning to end. Each shot would stand as a separate entity. They are somewhat like blackouts in Vaudeville. One segment has no image at all but is instead an edited art lecture in which a narrator describes ways to make an image "more interesting." By this time I had

Banana, 1975   Beverle Houston, 1975   Husky pups, 1973   Studio details, Los Angeles, 1980s

seen Peter Hutton's films. I think the first one I saw was *Images of Asian Music*. Bob Nelson introduced me to his work. Hutton uses no cuts, and the way this procedure sharpens attention to the individual parts was a revelation. Regarding Nelson, I had known Bob's work for a while, again, from Movies Around Midnight. We saw films like *Half Open and Lumpy* and *Oiley Pelosa and the Pumph Man*. Later I saw *The Great Blondino*, the long piece he did in collaboration with William Wiley. Then Bob taught at CalArts for a couple of years, 1972 and 1973 maybe. He made *Bleu Shut* around then.

Q: Can you talk a bit more about your motivations for the segmentation of *Saugus Series*?

A: *Saugus Series*, *Sidewinder's Delta* [1976], and *Foregrounds* [1978] are all segmented pieces. In fact, the idea was that the filmic segments could be shown individually as loops. They are open structures and do not necessarily have to be connected together, but they have always been shown from beginning to end.

With *Saugus Series* I begun with setups. I shot into a water tank in time-lapses to reveal the reflection of the sun moving across the water's surface. Another section is timed by a man sawing a tree branch. There are objects that are painted repeatedly with a spray gun—images appear and are painted over and replaced by others. A pair of shoes changes color. I also made a shot by pouring black roofer's asphalt over a glass surface mounted in front of a blue-screen backing. The result was repeated three times laterally to make a three-colored ripple that moves like a waterfall down a geological formation that seems at first like roasting meat. The mountain is actually a geyser in Yellowstone. This segment is accompanied by a tune from a Chinese recording that imparts an upbeat ceremonial quality to the whole undertaking.

As the film goes on, it becomes flatter and less representational. A handheld shot of Joshua trees interrupts as a continuous field of stripes. Toward the end of the film there is a field of moving dots and lines, many, many superimpositions. At the very end there is a floating object—a man's hat floating on water—that crosses the screen. This was during the Watergate Era, and the hat with a stingy brim was George Mitchell's.

Q: Is the abstraction in *Saugus Series* always maintained in tension with the real, the photographic?

A: Yes, that pairing of opposites is very important. I need one to mark the other.

Q: You have described *Saugus Series* as a complex and sensual visual text. You create a fluid surface out of diverse visual sources. You utilize recurring strategies of appropriation, collage, and assemblage. As you were making this work and as you encounter it today, what are the various meanings of these visual elements and techniques?

A: Well, the falls sequence is about glamour and sensuality. The asphalt moves slowly and constantly reshapes itself. And there are three stripes, like a well-rehearsed trio of backup singers. Undercutting that is the background, which is steamy in another sense entirely, like watching ducks cooking in a Chinese restaurant's window.

Q: Is there irony in this?

A: Yes. Think of the mountain as the logo for Paramount Pictures and think about the glamorous women that appear at the Academy Awards. I try to restate an impression using very different materials. I suppose everything in *Saugus Series* is sort of place and process bound. The primary colors are about the laboratory process. The source of the image is dyes on film.

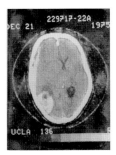

Brain scan, 1975   Pat O'Neill at UCLA Medical Center, 1976   Pat O'Neill at Victoria, B.C., 1976   Joan Logue and Beverly O'Neill, 1976

Q: Is the composition of the film's sequences done quickly? Do you put elements together intuitively or do you sketch them out in advance?

A: I find that previsualization usually yields only a rough approximation of what a finished piece will become. I begin with the assumption that whatever I am working on will change, sometimes drastically, before it is completed. In fact, the senses of its completeness is often subject to revision. The way one works—the preparation, the way elements are laid out, conditions in the studio, and most importantly, conditions in the mind—will have a bearing on how I work. It seems, on a good night at least, that the pieces make themselves. Each one will present its own set of rules, and each act alters all that went before. Solutions often cannot be coaxed, but appear spontaneously.

Perhaps what I am doing is making objects that act as training exercises for an audience, in a particular way of seeing, of relating to the world. The "world" is, after all, far more absurd and vastly more unjust than one can begin to represent. It is necessary to acknowledge these perilous circumstances while taking pleasure in small gifts of the day-to-day, that this is what I try to do.

It is also worth mentioning that all of this goes on under the long shadow of "Art History"—calling for the recognition that, today, nothing is new, there is no new, unbroken ground, that one is simply rearranging, cheerfully, the common legacy of image-making

Q: I don't remember seeing much use of language in your films. Am I right?

A: Well, in *Saugus Series* there is a section that is spoken. But I didn't use text as a visual element until *Water and Power* [1989].

Q: Before we leave the 1970s, let's talk about *Sidewinder's Delta*. It has color strips and disorientating upside down shots of Monument Valley.

Aspects of the film reminded me of Brakhage's *Text of Light*, and I was also intrigued by your use of the Western landscape. Can you describe the shift that took place in this work in your approach to abstraction?

A: In *Sidewinder's Delta* I was starting to work with direct emulsion processes: painting and scratching on film, making complex combinations of simple, handmade elements. And it was during the making of *Sidewinder's Delta*—two weeks after I had resigned from CalArts—that I was hospitalized with an aneurysm, a blood clot on the brain. It was 1975, Christmastime. I went into a coma that lasted for ten days. When I regained consciousness, I learned that I had survived brain surgery. All the parts seemed to work, except that I found myself looking at a *New Yorker* cartoon, and it had something under it, and I looked at it and said, "What's that?" I realized it was text, but I had no idea what it meant. Gradually my perceptions began to settle in, but for a while it was similar to some of the film work I had done—the surface was interrupted. People have drawn a connection between my illness and this tendency in my filmmaking, but I was working that way before it happened and continued doing so after.

Gradually I could read a bit. I worked for a year and a half with a tutor to relearn reading, but I never got beyond about fifty words a minute. I couldn't read fast enough to keep up with film subtitles. When I go to a foreign-language film I only look at the visuals, or rely on someone to whisper in my ear. I can read an article if I sit down for hours. In the scale of things, I was incredibly lucky to survive. You deal with it. When there is time, Bev reads to me and rents foreign films to provide me with the voiceover.

Q: Your work is definitely in dialogue with what's being written and made today. Structural and poststructural theory is grounded in language. Your work is grounded in the visual, the treatment and re-treatment of the visual, from the found image to generated

Single head optical printer, CalArts, 1972   Double head optical printer, Lookout Mountain, 1990   Greg Ercolano at work, 1990

abstraction. So your work both invites and resists the language model. How do you write about and describe the moving image, which is constantly changing? Embodied in your work is a whole set of very interesting visual challenges to language-based interpretation.

A: I guess I've chosen to attempt things that might fail, to bring things together that raise problems. I am fascinated by things that seem a little foolish, a little ugly. I remember seeing my first Bruce Nauman sculpture at the Wilder Gallery in the early sixties. He was making fiberglass representations of the spaces between the furniture in his house. He wall-mounted these awkward, rough triangles and parallelograms. I thought they were the dumbest objects I'd ever seen. But they raised the question of why one makes any object. They presented a problem that insisted on an answer.

Q: You are pointing to a still from *Sidewinder's Delta*. How does it exemplify the potent awkwardness you are describing?

A: In *Sidewinder's Delta* I took roles of 16mm leader and attacked them with a sharp object, making a lot of clumsy marks. The printing master that followed had all of these marks built into it, and each time it was exposed it revealed another increment of the background image, which is a shot of dissolving and flowing paint on a vertical surface. I keep going back to printing technology to see how it can be used to create complex surfaces.

Q: *Sidewinder's Delta* shows the hand in and on the landscape. This is a subjective assessment on my part, but do you think this moment, or others in the film, express a state of melancholy?

A: That's one strain, one part of it, for sure. The landscape is Monument Valley, which references the West and Western film—John Ford, *Stagecoach*, and, of course, the people who live there, the Navajo. I traveled there in awe, and for many years did no shooting at all. It seemed almost disrespectful to photograph there: I was drawn to be there, but felt I had nothing to add to its representation. Finally, in the early seventies, I spent a period of time there, recorded a few observations, and executed a piece which involved placing sheets of colored paper into the predominantly red environment. Later, the colors of those sheets could be replaced, presenting a bogus demonstration of a "Chameleonic" substance. This was followed by a Saguaro cactus, which would, when shown colored light, spontaneously change its color to the opposite side of the spectrum, making it stand out from its surroundings. I shot the Mitten Butte in its upright position and then briefly inverted it. I was interested in the way an image reassembles itself when you look at it upside down. More recently I have paid attention to this in a series of small, agitated drawings made with a constantly shifting orientation. We always search for clues to orient ourselves in the space of a drawing. Each time we rotate a drawing ninety degrees new clues emerge to make it totally different. Space entirely depends on what story we tell ourselves.

Q: Did video attract you at all?

A: I thought it was a useful way to document something but never found the image quality to be satisfactory. I also crave the scale and the darkness of the theater. For the last ten years I have been shooting on Hi-8 and then mini DV, but I have never finished a work in that format. I blew up a few minutes shot on a train in Germany and included it in *Trouble in the Image*.

Q: This description of your process is very interesting. In the 1970s people were reading Morse Peckham's book *Man's Rage for Chaos*. He wrote about the issue of human expectation. I think that resides in your work and in your process.

A: Chaos is particularly the operating principle in *Let's Make a Sandwich* [1978]. It

Edition of buttons, 1977

is a projection installation. Whenever it's shown, I say, "if you can stay with this for one minute out of twenty, that's all you need to do. I am interested in the images you make in your mind." I was trying to take found footage to an extreme of disintegration. After I had superimposed as many as twenty layers through several generations, I wanted to find out what was left of the original images. I tried to make a film that used every conceivable kind of material—stuff shot off television, New York City in a snowstorm, an aquarium, zoo animals, cartoons, training films. I put it together without regard to content or even right side up or down. I repeatedly superimposed rolls over one another until I had a continually moving field. At times you see perspectival illusions, caricatures, figures in motion, grids, bits of lettering. The original content has been boiled down until it almost disappears, but not quite—that's the trick.

Let's Make a Sandwich was a kind of summation. I initially showed it in a very large room at LACE (Los Angeles Contemporary Exhibitions).

Q: How was it projected?
A: It was a loop projector with a rear projection screen hanging free out in the room. It was the only piece I showed, and the room was a good eighty feet square. You could walk around and see it from a distance or up close. It was shown continuously, day and night, for five days. The experience can be likened to Stan Vander Beek's Theater of Dreams. Exhaustion, boredom, and distraction can actually help you to reach a film.

Q: What about your film Foregrounds, also from 1978?
A: Foregrounds is a segmented piece continuing on from Sidewinder's Delta. Perhaps its most memorable section is the last one. A short loop of film is seen hanging on a tree branch. It is in motion; action is visible in the individual frames of the film. Moving closer, the action is revealed to be a tracking shot of palm trees moving from left to right. It is about the projector, the intermittent movement, and the filmstrip, all displayed in the unfamiliar confines of an overgrown garden.

Q: How did Lookout Mountain Films come about and what is its relationship to your films?
A: After making 7362, I was approached to do photographic effects work for commercials. I worked for a number of production houses beginning in 1969, making various arrangements to use optical printers. I began to teach at CalArts in 1970, when it was founded, and for a time I did my own film work on the school's equipment. In 1974, I was able to obtain a vintage single-head printer of my own. It took ten years and a lot of jobs to pay it off. I converted our garage into a studio and named the company after the street we lived on—Lookout Mountain Avenue—because I liked the sound of it. We did work on feature films by Haile Gerima, Donna Deitch, Will Vinton, Larry Clark, and Melvin Van Peebles. We did commercial projects of all kinds—titles, archival stuff, and effects shots. I could colorize shots and do some background replacement. We got a rotoscoping stand so we could project material and do wire removal from acrobatic stunts. In 1980, we got hooked up with Lucasfilm and did a lot of work on the second and third movies in the Star Wars trilogy.

Q: You were active in the film collective Oasis. Can you discuss what this group meant to the independent film culture in Los Angeles?
A: Oasis was started in 1976 by Grahame Weinbren and Roberta Freidman, who were a filmmaking couple at the time. Beverly and I joined in the effort, as did Amy Halpren, who had just come from the Collective for Living Cinema in New York, Morgan Fisher, David and Diana Wilson, Paul Arthur, and Tom Leeser. We wanted to present touring filmmakers and exhibit work that otherwise would not

Felice Mataré and Carl Cheng, c. 2001   Drawing, hotel room, Tampere, Finland, 1998   Pat O'Neill and Bill Moritz, 1980   Chick Strand and Marty Muller, 1972

appear in Southern California. We did the first screenings at an old lefty theater called the Haymarket. Our very first event was a presentation of Jonas Mekas's *Lithuanian Diaries*. After a year we moved to LAICA, the Los Angeles Institute for Contemporary Art, an alternative gallery on Robertson Boulevard. Every Sunday night we would arrive with the projector, screen, chairs, and programs, do a screening, and then pack up. We operated as a collective. Everybody who contributed their time could bring in screening proposals. When we showed Warhol's *Chelsea Girls*, which is a two-screen piece, nearly 250 people packed into the gallery. I am sure it was totally illegal. Oasis remained active until 1982 when worker fatigue took its toll and the group disbanded.

Q: What was your perception of Structural film on the West Coast?
A: I first encountered Michael Snow's *Wavelength* in Gene Youngblood's screenings at CalArts, along with Ken Jacobs's *Tom Tom the Piper's Son*, and Ernie Gehr's *Serene Velocity*. At first these works seemed totally puzzling. Why does one make such an object? Are we to look at, or just read about it? And how have these ideas come to have such authority in other academic settings? These works threw out all of the baggage of past cinemas, and wasn't it time that happened? In fact, our own ideas began to look quaint, indulgent, and inadequate. I was struggling to relate. Over time I came to terms with the ideas of Materialist filmmaking, even to feel an affinity for the way these long, dry projects explained their assumptions, given patience and repeated screenings. Was it time to acknowledge that one's practice had simply been made obsolete? Not only was I surrounded by the indifferent milieu of Hollywood, but also the sense of possibility I had felt in the underground seemed to have evaporated.

Q: What happened then?
A: I cultivated the garden, painted our VW. I had begun to assimilate some new

notions of temporality, as could be seen in the real-time duration of *Two Sweeps* [1979] and even as far back as *Down Wind*'s interruptive geometry. And I realized that the structuralist model supported only so many iterations and had perhaps already shown signs of exhaustion. It was an interesting period in retrospect, perhaps the last time that a critical imperative carried such weight and generated such discussion. It addressed film as form rather than as a vehicle for content, and that discussion has been very muted ever since.

Q: What did you think of Snow's work?
A: The first time I saw *La Region Centrale*, I didn't watch it through to the end. The second time I did, and I was profoundly affected. The view to the empty landscape is completely about the way the camera moves. By the end of three and a half hours looking at the screen you become identified with the camera, at least I did. I felt like the whole theater was moving. It seemed like the most effective dance film I'd ever seen. It's choreography for the camera. That was an influence that led me to make *Water and Power*, which moves in a more limited way but also uses scores that define the motion of the camera. Motion control allowed me to take a multiplicity of shots which all had the identical motion. I photographed widely different subjects and combined them in the optical printer.

Q: Let's focus on the body of work that constitutes your production in the last two decades, beginning with *Water and Power*, which was the first time you made a film in 35mm.
A: I began *Water and Power* in 1982. I teamed up with Mark Madel, an artist and filmmaker who wrote software for me that could motion-control a camera. It was an ingenious invention that used one of the first portable computers. It made it possible to drive four axes: pan, tilt, zoom, and exposure. I wanted to make the moves in the shots repeatable—that was the heart of the whole thing. I wanted to

Pat and Beverly O'Neill with Hollis Frampton, 1977

CLOCKWISE (FROM TOP LEFT): Grahame Weinbren, 1980; Pat O'Neill with Tom Leeser, 1995; Diana and David Wilson, 1978; Bill Moritz, 1970; Roberta Friedman, 1977; Nicolas Bautista and Marsha Kinder, 1978

shoot something on location and then go back and recreate the movement in the studio, shooting miniatures, an interior, or actors. It is something I have been fascinated with for years because I was shooting a lot of time-lapses, making an exposure every five seconds or every twenty seconds to record the movement of sunlight. In order to do that the camera was always stationary. I knew about motion-control from the industry and from working on commercials but had never actually shot this way or even used a computer.

I spent a lot of time in Owens Valley, northeast of Los Angeles. It once was an agricultural zone beginning in the 1880s. It was bought by the Los Angeles Department of Water and Power and was the site of the major water importation that allowed the city to expand after 1915. As the Owens Valley water table was dropping, some farmers tried to hold out and keep their land. In the 1920s, the aqueduct was blown up a couple of times, but gradually the farmers gave up. I was drawn to the area, not because of politics, but because of its remarkable geography. Alongside this valley runs the highest mountains in the country. When you are in the Owens Valley, the Eastern Sierra is a wall of 12,000 to 14,000-foot peaks. The valley goes down to a 3,000-foot elevation and then to the east there is another range of mountains. So basically it's this long rift.

Q: It mirrors the horizontal lines you love in your films.

A: Right. And at the bottom of the valley there is a lakebed that is primarily dry, a bed made of soda ash and salt crystals. There is some cattle ranching and the remains of a mining culture that began in the 1870s. There was a lot of silver, lead, and zinc taken out of the mines up in the mountains at Cerro Gordo, and a lot of waste products spread out and contaminated the valley. Because of these high mountains and this deep valley, there is a shadow that moves across like a sundial. It writes the exposure change on the valley's floor. I got interested in using this moving shadow as a thematic divider, almost like a wipe. I shot the

valley from different perspectives—long pans on the floor and from the vantage point of a road that goes up into the Sierras. I supplemented this material with shots from Twin Peaks in San Francisco, to get residential neighborhoods. I shot a lot in Bolinas, up in Marin County, and in downtown Los Angeles. I rented a studio at 6th and Main and shot off the roof to get panoramic views of the city. And inside I set up a blacked-out environment in which to record performers.

Q: A theme in this conversation has been the complexity of your image—its diversity, movement, and change. *Water and Power* exemplifies how you function as a bricoleur who combines and unites fragments to a smooth finish. Yet this degree of complexity resists interpretation. What are the key terms that define *Water and Power* for you?

A: I wanted to make naturalistic landscapes that were filled with contradictions. One shot that I particularly like is near the middle of the film. It moves over a neighborhood. Gradually the pan discovers a person who is seen from the shoulders up. He is eating a meal and talking. You move across his profile. You can still see the neighborhood, you can see him, and you come to a tabletop that is cluttered with debris. Among the debris is a plaster sculpture, a little dog with its head missing. You move past the tabletop and into a window in the room. The window is reflecting the light. The light goes off and you begin to see through it. You move back out of the room and see the city at night. So you have found this person in this room with these artifacts. Among them is a neon sign that spells out the word "nuts" in red letters. But it is reflected in a mirror so that the word "nuts" appears as "stun." The pan captures a place where a person exists. I am always trying to balance content so that it does not become soley about a specific person, job, or neighborhood. I am trying to make it both general and specific at the same time.

Owens Lake, California, 1984

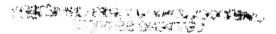

Q: Did you use found footage in *Water and Power*?

A: I shot almost everything in *Water and Power*, but there is some found footage with references to early Hollywood. There is footage from Cecil B. De Mille's 1926 *Ten Commandments*. The scene is of a vast crowd of people and Moses stands before them and directs them to go to where the Red Sea had parted.

Q: In my notes, I describe the performers as looking like George Segal sculptures. There is a similarity, I think, in that the figures you film are frozen, or nearly frozen, in time. You mold a representation of time out of these people as they repeat an action.

A: Segal was a reference, particularly on my last film, *The Decay of Fiction*. I showed the actors some images of Segal's work to help them realize that it wasn't about total naturalism, that their work would be seen in a different way.

Q: Describe some other scenes that illustrate particular techniques and goals that you had in *Water and Power*.

A: Towards the end there is a sequence that focuses on an urban neighborhood. It happens to be San Francisco, seen from the top of Twin Peaks. I made a very repetitive camera move—a rectangle that always returns to the same point. I wanted to tell a story with inter-titles. It is a description of a woman in a room. She emerges from the shower and a bullet comes through the window. She drops to the floor and crawls to look out the window. There does not seem to be anyone out there. While this is going on, the camera is moving right to left, top to bottom, left to right, bottom to top. It repeatedly makes a square while looking at a hillside with houses and busy streets. And it is fast enough so that the image is strobing a bit. Basically I made the shot repetitively all afternoon, changing the zoom lens' focal length from time to time, so that sometimes it is covering a small area and seems to be moving fast, and sometimes it is covering a wide area and seems to be moving slower.

Q: What drew you to that scene, to that story, to that action?

A: I was trying to recreate some of the tension of film noir. I wrote the material, but it is so generic it could have come from anything of the period. I wanted to evoke an incident entirely through written words, while the camera's searching movement reinforces it in a non-descriptive way. This is a technique I have used as far back as *Runs Good*. I try to give the part of the mind that uses language something to do. I strip the film of conventional grammar and replace it with something else. To deprive the audience entirely of narrative in a long film is a real risk.

Q: It seems to me that the hermeneutic challenge of your work lies in an absorbingly rich and seamless use of source material. You have forged a juncture between visual fecundity and stylistic fluidity. This allows your work to maintain mystery and ambiguity.

A: All I can say is that, to me, it resembles life. Every interaction is full of unspoken knowledge. Every moment is full of memories of the past and expectations of the future. There is always your mind's eye *and* what you are actually seeing. All experience is a composite: someone could tell you something and while you are being told that, maybe you are hearing music on the radio and looking outside and seeing a girl bend over and pick up her glasses. You track all those things at once. But in narrative, the story takes control, the rest is background. Storytelling is inevitably linear.

Q: Your work represents the world as multi–textual, multilayered. You tangibly depict the complexities of cognition, or epistemology, how we understand the world. We have talked some about duration, and

Owens Valley, California, 1984

I'm curious if you feel your work shares a rapport with someone like Bill Viola who also deals with temporal issues—narrative time, perceptual time, historical time.

A: He slows actions down so you see a range of movement and expression that you would never catch in real time. I have done similar things with landscape, revealing an experience that you normally can't perceive. I was particularly affected by *Room for St. John of the Cross* in which drastically different modes of representation seem to stand for inner and outer life.

Q: What about your film *Trouble in the Image*, from 1996? It seems to have earlier footage. Can you explain how it came about?

A: Some of it was shot for *Water and Power* and even before. It is really a series of separate studies, a studio practice film. I call it "works on film from 1975 to 1996."

Q: What do you mean by that?

A: I sometimes like to realize an idea quite quickly, to respond to found material, or to go into the studio and film myself doing an action. I might make live-action shots to add to existing backgrounds, or freely animated line drawings. Overtime these materials accumulate. I wanted a structure that could contain some of them and began to conceive of it as clusters of three shots each triads, with each of the three shots very different from one another. Within each group is diversity, but between the clusters are similarities. I wound up with about thirty such groupings, which I arranged blindly, using a random number table. Then George Lockwood and I started in on the soundtrack. The track was made primarily of re-used dialogue fragments and music. It also includes readings of my own written fragments. George would digitize the material and edit in a digital studio. His musician's ear led to many surprising refinements in the editing process. The track was entirely spatial, which is revealed in the rare projections with an optimized stereo system.

Q: Do you think of yourself as an abstract artist or a conceptual artist, or neither?

A: I would say I work abstractly, in that meaning for me has more to do with the relationship between parts than the individual parts themselves. But I retain an oblique connection to narrative and storytelling.

Q: Your images are loaded with semantic meaning. They all have associations.

A: I enjoy regarding recognizable images as formal entities and perceiving them abstractly. The problem is finding a balance between what one knows about the subject matter and what one sees.

Q: How did you come to the title for your film *Coreopsis* [1998]?

A: *Coreopsis* is named after a little yellow daisy. I was working with something that was mostly yellow, and it reminded me of those blossoms. In my mother's personal things there was an old envelope of seeds, which she had labeled "Coreopsis—Helen, 1935." That's her sister. I knew my folks had been in Nebraska in 1935, and I found it interesting that viable seeds could be saved for so many years, so I named the film after the flower.

Coreopsis is one of the scratch films I made in the mid- to late-1990s. They were quick exercises and used a frame-reordering procedure I call a progressive loop. This was something that David LeBrun employed in a film called *Tanka* [1970], which is an amazing piece. He made a printing scheme for the optical printer where he would duplicate seven frames forward and then back up the original six frames and repeat this throughout the shot. This makes a repetition, but it's an ever-changing one. You can come up with any pattern—say twelve forward and five back. The more you repeat, the more rhythmic it is, and the more you advance, the more freeform it is. I improvised on the printer, changing the patterns randomly.

Coreopsis is basically thirty feet of scribed leader. If you scratch into black leader made on color-print film with a scribe, it removes the black and leaves behind some yellow and green. The point will pick up everything but the cyan. If you take that off you have yellow. If you take everything off you have clear. When you put scratched film in the printer and put light through it, the clear portions are brighter and produce an expanded line. You get a size gradation from bright to dark. I would take a strip of film with me and draw on it from time to time.

Q: The colors in *Coreopsis* are extraordinary, and the forms you scratched in are linear but also almost biomorphic. Do you relate this type of work to Brakhage's hand-painted films?
A: Yes, certainly. I have been thinking about the way Stan evolved into this working process. For me the limitation of direct drawing is its complexity and speed. There is more visual information coming at you than you can take in. I wanted to be able to fix on and consider certain forms, and that's why I decided to establish repetitive cycles.

Q: We have talked about different kinds of associations that have narrative meaning but resist an overall narrative structure. Your most recent work, *The Decay of Fiction*, is structured by a building in which people circulate, and by an extraordinary soundtrack. While it is clearly related to your past work, it is also very distinctive. Could you talk about how it came into being?
A: It definitely came out of *Water and Power*. In the early 1990s I was looking around for another location. I was interested in finally undertaking the direction of actors. Since I hadn't done it for so many years, it was sort of like the elephant sitting in the corner.

Q: But you had directed gestures....
A: Yes, but never dialogue. I was worried about taking on sync sound. I was concerned narrative would pre-empt other formal concerns that I wanted to retain. The first thing I did was to have a new motion-control system made that was capable of running the camera at twenty-four frames-per-second, which meant that it had a much larger memory and could move the camera around much more quickly. The Ambassador Hotel came to me out of the blue, like most things do. I knew it was vacant. Donald Trump and some other investors owned the building and planned to tear it down to build a very tall office building. This was in 1988. At the same time, the Board of Education attempted to seize the property under eminent domain. So the two parties got involved in litigation that lasted ten years. I went to visit in 1993. At first I saw the building like a natural formation, like a sandstone ridge reflecting the sunlight. And the place was also historically significant. There were stories around every corner.

There is an aura to a spot with a strong collective memory attached to it. The Ambassador was built in 1920 as a luxury hotel and was very much part of the movie industry. The first Academy Awards were held there. The reporter Walter Winchell lived there when he was in Los Angeles. J. Edgar Hoover lived there part-time when he was director of the FBI. John Kennedy stayed there a number of times. Robert Kennedy was assassinated at the Ambassador in June 1968.

Q: What was the production process? Did you begin with a script and storyboards? Where did the stories come from?
A: Initially I studied the spaces to determine how they were revealed by sunlight at specific times of day. I gradually built a list of locations whose light I wanted to capture and places, such as the ballroom, that needed to be lit. I used a stopwatch to time shots so that they could contain scenes. At this point, the scenes themselves had not been written, but I knew, for example, that I wanted to

Production Detail, *The Decay of Fiction*, March 2001   Production Detail, *The Decay of Fiction*, March 2001

pan across a patio as the shadow of the adjacent building crept across its tiled floor. I knew how long it would take someone to walk the length of a hallway, so we could design a camera move that would follow her. George Lockwood and I filmed at the hotel for a year and a half, off and on. Eventually we had about four hours of footage. I began preparing a rough cut and planning the action. My research consisted of looking at noir films on tape. In my imagination the hotel had become firmly located in that historic zone. My job was to adapt or re-imagine scenes from dozens of sources to fit the shots we had made.

In 1999 we started casting. I put an ad in a *Drama-Logue* asking for a man of a certain age, a woman of a certain age, thinking I might get a handful of people. I got 3,800 headshots in the mail. We needed a large dark space to shoot the action so we used the hotel's convention hall. We took the dimensions of the shots and put markers on the floor for actors to follow. The shoot lasted six weeks. *The Decay of Fiction* is the most thematically contained piece I've ever done. We did a document of a site, showing it exactly the way we I found it and then transplanting a fictive population into it.

Q: Can you talk about the segments with small figures and other details in relation to the ending?
A: Yes, there are seven short sequences which prefigure the film's last movement. They often occur in small-scale models with drastically scaled-down humans. I began making these shots late in the editing process, when I had nearly finished the core of the optical composites. I began with primitive animations, building with fragments and scraps of leftover trinkets such as might have been found in the empty building—lightbulbs, dolls ports, broken things. These sections inserted another voice or consciousness into the film, commenting upon or I wanted to step backward—or forward—to childhood. Characters on their way to a big

costume gala come down the hallway from all directions and defy the architecture, emerging through the walls. The space opens up to reveal a stage of indeterminate depth. People cross through one another and other images penetrate them. This section succumbs gradually to the lure of uncertainty. The fiction of the proceeding sequences disappears just as the particulars of the individuals in these shots become more pungent. Characters reappear, frequently wearing different disguises. I have always felt that hotels were places for changing identities, or for revealing identities peculiarly our own.

The end that I originally anticipated for the film involved the actual demolition of the building. The demolition was pending, but it became apparent that it wouldn't happen. We ultimately used recordings of a building demolition over the credits.

Q: It's also a film about illusion, isn't it? About Hollywood?
A: Yes, and it is also about the institution that thrives on creating illusions for other people. It's my way of describing Hollywood to someone who has no idea what it is. I didn't go there to eulogize it. I went there because it's an empty building that captures the light in interesting ways.

Q: But did you feel you had to resist being nostalgic?
A: No, I think I just dived into it, and into all of its implications. It's the artificiality of the culture that interests me—the immersion of the characters in their roles, contrasted with the inexorable rotation of the planet.

Q: With this film completed, has it caused you to think again about the trajectory of your work? What are you thinking about these days?
A: The expense of the last film made me think about doing very inexpensive projects, like drawing on film. I'm also thinking about doing more shooting with

George Lockwood in Ireland, 2001   County Wicklow, Ireland, 1999   Beverly O'Neill, 1985

performers. There are ideas involving with the human body in defined space that I think I haven't really finished with yet. We're at a point now where making composite moving images digitally is becoming affordable. Some days I think that the filmmaking part of my work is over and I'm just going to make still images for awhile—to let the viewer make the movement, make the journey using imagination.

Q: You made a DVD called *Tracing The Decay of Fiction: Encounters with a Film by Pat O'Neill*. How did it come about? Do you consider it a complete work separate from the film?

A: In 1999, about the time we were about to shoot the action, I showed Marsha Kinder some of the footage. She asked if I would be interested in working on an interactive project related to the film as part of the Annenberg Foundation's Labyrinth Project, where she is director. I realized I'd created a project ideally suited for a database structure. The parts are not connected in a linear way, and I liked the notion of a participant unfolding the material in an unpredictable way. It's a horizontal structure as opposed to a vertical one. The Labyrinth Project's mission is to provide digital opportunities for artists and authors who are not primarily working with computers. I brought in materials and ideas and collaborated with a computer programmer, Rosemary Comella, and a graphic designer, Kristy Kang.

I began thinking about what shape the project should take. I soon realized it should extend beyond the film and bring together lots of elements and evidence—history, anecdote, geography, and artifacts. So I took the dramatic or the semi-narrative material that we'd shot and put it side-by-side with archival material. We did research in archives for early photographs of the building's construction and records of notable events that took place there. We met Carolyn Benjamin, a wonderful storyteller, whose father was hotel manager from 1920 to 1938. We found people who had witnessed the Kennedy assassination. We synthe-

sized their stories with written material about the aftermath of the assassination and the investigations that followed. There were a number of sources, including state historian Kevin Starr had a lot to say about the significance of the Wilshire corridor and why the hotel was put there.

The DVD ended up incorporating a quarter of the film combined with a couple hours of other material. It's an introduction to the idea of the film, but you could certainly experience it without seeing the film. It's a hybrid.

Q: A new generation of moving-image makers is working in film and video installation, interactive work, and performance. Are you aware of this work and do you feel a connection to it? The independent film culture, which has been central to our entire conversation, has evaporated as we knew it—the supports, funding, and distribution. Increasingly you see people projecting something on a wall in a gallery and trying to put their work into that economy of support.

A: It's gratifying for that to become a possibility. I've experienced installations by artists like Grahame Weinbren, Douglas Gordon, Pipilotti Rist, Sharon Lockhart, Christian Marclay, Jennifer Steinkamp, Erika Suderburg, and George Stone, to name a few. I've found much there to like. The success of these artists indicates that this new genre has taken root.

Q: Do you have any interest in returning to the installation format?

A: We are soon going to begin putting up a building here that will allow me, for the first time, to plan room-size, three-dimensional projects in which actions can be both filmed and projected. It is something I have been trying to get underway for years, and I am excited about what may follow.

Pat O'Neill, 2004

CHRONOLOGY

1939
Born Los Angeles

1964
MA, University of California, Los Angeles (UCLA)

1965
Married Beverly Morris

1966
One-person exhibition, Orlando Gallery, Encino, California

1968
"Plastics: L.A." Esther Robles Gallery, Los Angeles
"NOW Technology in Art," Esther Robles Gallery, Los Angeles
7362 included in Ann Arbor Film Festival

1969
Group show, "Electric Art," curated by Oliver Andrews

1970
Moves to Laurel Canyon; founding faculty at California Institute of the Arts (CalArts)
Group show, "A Plastic Presence" organized by Gerald Nordland, toured to the Jewish Museum, Milwaukee Art Center, and San Francisco Museum of Modern Art

1971
Runs Good receives First Prize at Ann Arbor Film Festival

1974
Founding of Lookout Mountain Films

1975
Survives cerebral hemorrhage

1976
American Film Institute filmmaker grant; founding of Oasis, an independent film screening collaborative

1978
Installation, *Let's Make a Sandwich,* LACE, Los Angeles

1979
Installation, *Two Sweeps,* in group show curated by Grahame Weinbren, Mount San Antonio College, Walnut, California

1984
Begins production of *Water and Power*

1985
National Endowment Grant in Film for *Water and Power;* "20-20," twentieth-anniversary exhibition for UCLA's Photography Department, Los Angeles

1989
Water and Power premieres at Experimental Film Congress, Toronto

1990
Water and Power invited to Berlin Film Festival; *Water and Power* receives Jury prize for documentary, Sundance Film Festival, Salt Lake City, Colorado
James Phelan Award, Film Arts Foundation, San Francisco

1991
Water and Power included in Whitney Biennial, Whitney Museum of American Art, New York

1992
Guggenheim Fellowship in Filmmaking, Solomon R. Guggenheim Museum, New York; retrospective of film work, Paris Film Archive, Paris

1993
Maya Deren Award for Independent Filmmaking, lifetime achievement, American Film Institute (AFI), awarded at Anthology Film Archive, New York

1994
Begins production on *The Decay of Fiction*

1996
Water and Power included in "Art and Film Since 1945: Hall of Mirrors" at The Museum of Contemporary Art, Los Angeles; *Trouble in the Image* premieres at Los Angeles County Museum of Art with live performance by George Lockwood and musicians of *Let's Make a Sandwich* and *Two Sweeps*

1997
Rockefeller Foundation Grant for *The Decay of Fiction;* retrospective of film work, Pesaro Film Festival, Rome

1998
Retrospective of film work, European Media Arts Festival, Osnabruck, Germany; "Mister Exacto: Carl Cheng and Pat O'Neill, Photographic Work," University of Nevada, Reno, Nevada

1999
One-person exhibition of digital composite prints, Gallery Luisotti, Santa Monica, California

2002
Tracing The Decay of Fiction: Encounters with a Film by Pat O'Neill, interactive DVD, collaboration with The Labyrinth Project, released by The Annenberg Center, University of Southern California, Los Angeles; "Future Cinema: The Cinematic Imaginary After Film," ZKM, Karlsruhe, Germany

2003
The Decay of Fiction premieres at the Getty Museum, Los Angeles; invited to "Views from the Avant Garde," New York Film Festival, New York; Rotterdam Film Festival, Rotterdam; London Film Festival, London; Pesaro Film Festival, Rome; Hong Kong Film Festival, Hong Kong; Image Forum, Tokyo; Film Festival, Seoul; Austrian Film Archive, Vienna; New Zealand Film Festival, Auckland; Danish Film Archive, Copenhagen; Athens Film Festival, Athens; retrospective of film work, The Art Gallery of Ontario, Toronto; award for *The Decay of Fiction,* OutFest, Los Angeles; Persistence of Vision Award, San Francisco Film Festival, San Francisco; performance of live sound versions of *Let's Make a Sandwich, Two Sweeps,* and *Horizontal Boundaries* (work-in-progress), Toronto Film Festival; *Easyout* and *Two Sweeps* included in "The Turbulent Screen," Edith Russ Haus, Oldenberg, Germany

2004
Invited to Viper Film Festival, Basel; invited to Istanbul Film Festival, Istanbul; Los Angeles Film Critics Association Award for Experimental Film; invited to Northwest Film Studies Center, Portland; invited Australian Center for the Moving Image, Melbourne

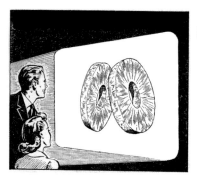

FILMOGRAPHY

The Decay of Fiction, 2002
35mm, 74 minutes, color, sound
Producer, Director, Editor: Pat O'Neill
Producer: Rebecca Hartzell
Assistant Producer: Nancy Oppenheim
Director of Photography: George Lockwood
Gaffer: Amy Halpern
Sound Design: George Lockwood
Optical Printer Operator: Kate McCabe
Cast (abridged): Wendy Winburn, Jack Conley, Lisa Moncure,
Patricia Thielemann, Jacqueline Humbert, and Damon Collazo
Ambassador Hotel Property Manager: Steve Lawlor
Pages 100–101; 186–87; 192

**Tracing The Decay of Fiction: Encounters with
a Film by Pat O'Neill,** 2002
The Labyrinth Project with Pat O'Neill
Projected interactive DVD-ROM installation
Digital media, projectors, sound system, computers
Dimensions variable
Executive Producer: Marsha Kinder
Directors: Rosemary Comella and Kristy H.A. Kang
with Pat O'Neill
Concept Design: Rosemary Comella, Kristy H.A. Kang,
Marhsa Kinder, and Pat O'Neill
Interface Design: Rosemary Comella and Kristy H.A. Kang
Sound Design: George Lockwood and Adam King
Production Manager: Priscilla Peña Ovalle
Assistant Producers: Nsenga K. Burton, JoAnn Hanley,
Alison Trope, and Cristina Venegas
Programming: Rosemary Comella
Digital Compositing and Graphic Design: Kristy H.A. Kang
Sound Engineer: Christopher Cain
Digital Media Compression: Priscilla Peña Ovalle
Video Production and Editing: Liang-yin Kuo and Tania Trepanier
Research and Rights Clearance: Myrton Running Wolf
Additional Sound Editing: Robyn Kali Bacon, Stefanos Kafatos,
Liang-yin Kuo, and Myrton Running Wolf
Additional Artwork: Scott Mahoy, Ariel McNichol, and
Priscilla Peña Ovalle
©2002 Annenberg Center for Communication, University
of Southern California
Funding Support: Annenberg Center for Communication,
University of Southern California; Southern California Study
Center (SC2), University of Southern California; The James
Irvine Foundation
Pages 190–91

Coreopsis, 1998
35mm, 6 minutes, color, silent
Pages 136–37

Squirt Gun Step Print, 1998
35mm, 5 minutes, black-and-white, silent

Horizontal Boundaries, 1998–present
35mm, 25 minutes, color, silent
Work-in-progress

Trouble in the Image, 1996
35mm, 38 minutes, color, sound
Sound Design: George Lockwood
Pages 64–65

Water and Power, 1989
35mm, 55 minutes, color, sound
Sound Design: George Lockwood
Motion Control Software Design: Mark Madel
Optical Printer Operator: Beth Block
Pages 24–25

Foregrounds, 1979
16mm, 13 minutes, color, sound
Pages 150–51

Two Sweeps, 1979
16mm, 20 minutes, color, silent
Loop projection
Dimensions variable
Pages 160–61

Let's Make a Sandwich, 1978
16mm, 20 minutes, color, silent
Loop projection
Dimensions variable
Pages 112–13

Sleeping Dogs (Never Lie), 1978
16mm, 9 minutes, black-and-white/color, silent/sound

Sidewinder's Delta, 1976
16mm, 20 minutes, color, sound
Pages 140–41

Saugus Series, 1974
16mm, 18 minutes, color, sound
Pages 126–27

Down Wind, 1973
16mm, 15 minutes, color, sound
Sound Design: Stan Levine
Pages 106–107

Last of the Persimmons, 1972
16mm, 6 minutes, color, sound
Pages 172–73

Easyout, 1971
16mm, 9 minutes, color, sound
Sound Design: Stan Levine
Pages 96–97

Runs Good, 1970
16mm, 15 minutes, color, sound
Sounds contributed by Cisko Curtis
Pages 90–91

Screen, 1969
16mm, 4 minutes, color, silent
Loop projection
Dimensions variable
Pages 38–39

7362, 1967
16mm, 10 minutes, color, sound
Sound Design: Joseph Byrd
Pages 56–57

Bump City, 1964
16mm, 6 minutes, color, sound
Pages 76–77

By the Sea, 1963
16mm, 10 minutes, black-and-white, silent
Collaboration with Robert Abel
Pages 32–33

EXHIBITION CHECKLIST

Venice Series, 1960–61
Eight gelatin-silver prints (1–8 in series)
11 x 14 in., each
Pages 98–99 (1–6); 104 (7) 102 (8)

Atlantic Auto Wrecking Series, 1961
Four gelatin-silver prints (1–4 in series)
11 x 14 in., each
Page 28 (1); 29 (2–4)

Untitled (Downtown LA Series), 1961
Gelatin-silver prints (1–2)
11 x 14 in., each
Page 31

Untitled (Fun), 1963
Gelatin-silver print
11 x 14 in.
Page 30

See the Native Girls, 1963
Gelatin-silver print
16 x 20 in.
Collection of Gaby and Wilhelm Schuermann, Herzogenrath, Germany
Page 103

Untitled (Collage 1), 1965
Paper collage on illustration board
17 x 19 in.
Page 26

Untitled (Collage 2), 1965
Paper collage on illustration board
19 x 19 in.
Page 27

Untitled (25er), 1965
Gelatin-silver print
11 x 14 in.
Page 30

Untitled (Rose Parade), 1966
Gelatin-silver print
16 x 20 in.
Page 144

L'il Neverbetter, 1969–2003
Polyester laminate, wood, lacquer finish
32 x 23 x 20 in.
Page 48

Swoop, 1969–2003
Cast iron, wood, lacquer finish
53 x 38 x 24 in.
Page 49

Virinia Red, 1969–2003
Polyester laminate, wood, lacquer finish
32 x 49 x 49 in.
Pages 50–51

Untitled (Fish), 1974
Monochrome silver print
14 x 11 in.
Page 139

Untitled (Strips), 1974
35mm film mounted in glass, wood frame
17 x 23 in.
Page 152

Untitled (Head/Tail Strips), 1974
35mm print film mounted in glass, wood frame
17 x 23 in.
Page 153

Untitled (Marble), 1974
Gelatin-silver print
14 x 11 in.
Page 138

Untitled (Ruled/Scratch), 1975
35mm print film mounted in glass, wood frame
17 x 23 in.
Page 159

Let's Make a Sandwich, 1978
16mm film, 20 minutes, color, silent
Loop projection
Dimensions variable
Pages 112–13

Two Sweeps, 1979
16mm film, 20 minutes, color, silent
Loop projection
Dimensions variable
Pages 160–61

Untitled (Cathedral), 1980
Gelatin-silver print, paper collage mounted on glass,
wood frame
16 x 19 in.
Page 157

Untitled (Dingo 3), 1980
Gelatin-silver print, black-and-white photocopy,
paper collage
32 x 17 in.
Page 59

Untitled (Dingo 4), 1980
Gelatin-silver print, black-and-white photocopy,
paper collage
19 x 16 in.
Pages 58–59

Untitled (Torn Portrait), 1980
Gelatin-silver print mounted in glass, wood frame
16 x 19 in.
Collection of Gaby and Wilhelm Schuermann, Herzogenrath, Germany
Page 156

Dixie's Table, 1983
Inkjet print on paper
26 x 22 in.
Page 61

Untitled (Camera), 1983
Paper collage mounted in glass, wood frame
16 x 19 in.
Collection of Gaby and Wilhelm Schuermann, Herzogenrath, Germany
Page 155

Punch Me In, 1984
Cibachrome print
26 x 22 in.
Page 60

Untitled (China/Food), 1984
Paper collage mounted in glass, wood frame
16 x 19 in.
Page 158

Untitled, 1984
Graphite on paper
9 x 12 in. (unframed)
Page 40

Untitled, 1985
Graphite on paper
9 x 12 in. (unframed)
Page 40

Seated Coil, 1985
Inkjet print on paper
26 x 22 in.
Page 177

Untitled, 1986
Graphite on paper
9 x 12 in. (unframed)
Page 40

During Fall Too Blue, 1990
Inkjet print on paper
26 x 22 in.
Page 176

Patty (Car with Graffiti), 1990
Type C print
14 x 11 in.
Page 130

Remote Control, 1990
Inkjet print on paper
28 x 32 in.
Page 62

Twelve Chairs, 1990
Type C print
14 x 11 in.
Page 131

Untitled (Four Piles of Salt), 1990
Type C print
14 x 11 in.
Page 133

Bar Wall, Ajo, 1992
Type C print
14 x 11 in.
Page 180

Untitled (Overhead View of South Patio), 1993
Ambassador Hotel Series
Type C print
14 x 11 in.
Page 189

Untitled (Phone Boxes), 1993
Ambassador Hotel Series
Type C print
14 x 11 in.
Page 188

Untitled (detail, South Patio), 1993
Ambassador Hotel Series
Type C print
14 x 11 in.
Page 188

Untitled, 1994
Graphite on paper (1–5)
8 1/2 x 11 in. each (unframed)
Page 40 (1); 42 (2, 4); 36 (3); 41 (5)

Untitled, 1995
Graphite on paper (1–3)
8 1/2 x 11 in. each (unframed)
Untitled (3), 1995, collection of Gaby and Wilhelm Schuermann,
Herzogenrath, Germany
Page 42 (1, 3); 46 (2)

3XXX 21 (Sulfur), 1995
Type C print
14 x 11 in.
Page 132

Untitled (Spectrum), 1995
Color Xerox print mounted in glass, wood frame
16 x 19 in.
Page 154

Untitled, 1996
Graphite on paper (1–5)
8 1/2 x 11 in. each (unframed)
Page 43 (1–4); 44 (5)

Untitled 1 (excerpts from Trouble in the Image), 1996
Type C prints (mounted)
17 x 20 in.
Page 110

Untitled 4 (excerpts from Trouble in the Image), 1996
Type C prints (mounted)
17 x 20 in.
Page 111

Mother Loathed (The Bagpipes), 1997
Inkjet print on paper
46 x 36 in.
Page 134

Two Figures with Water Tower, 1997
Inkjet print on paper
26 x 22 in.
Page 181

Untitled, 1997
Graphite on paper
8 1/2 x 11 in. (unframed)
Page 44

Le Sabre, 1998
Inkjet print on paper
36 x 46 in.
Page 135

Coreopsis, 1998
35mm film transferred to digital, 6 minutes,
color, silent, looped, displayed on plasma screen
Pages 136–37

Downdraft, 1998
Inkjet print on paper (two panels)
44 x 32 in. each
Collection of Jacqueline Humbert and David Rosenboom, Valencia, California
Pages 78–79

Triumph of Flattery, 1998
Inkjet print on paper
44 x 36 in.
Page 128

Untitled, 1998
Graphite on paper (1–2)
8 1/2 x 11 in. each (unframed)
Page 44

Dance of the Pinheads, 1999
Inkjet print on paper
96 x 42 in.
Pages 80–81

Dry Lake Stack, 1999
Inkjet print on paper
24 x 76 in.
Page 109

Owens Valley Stack, 1999
Inkjet print on paper
24 x 76 in.
Page 108

Fat Tree, 1999
Inkjet print on paper
48 x 32 in.
Collection of Gaby and Wilhelm Schuermann, Herzogenrath, Germany
Page 174–75

Untitled, 2001
Graphite on paper (1–4)
8 1/2 x 11 in. (unframed)
Page 45

Bastard 1, 2002
Performance Series
Inkjet print on paper
36 x 21 in.
Pages 86–87

Costume Figures, Amsterdam, 2002
Performance Series
Inkjet print on paper
82 x 46 in.
Pages 146–47

Downhill Bob, 2002
Performance Series
Inkjet print on paper
36 x 21 in.
Pages 82–83

Dr. Pierce, 2002
Inkjet print on paper
22 x 26 in.
Page 105

Iceman, 2002
Performance Series
Inkjet print on paper
36 x 21 in.
Pages 84–85

Rembrandt with Man, 2002
Inkjet print on paper
54 x 46 in.
Page 145

Rocky Grant, Windows, 2002
Inkjet print on paper
42 x 44 in.
Page 34

Sweet Pea, 2002
Inkjet print on paper
36 x 48 in.
Page 37

Swordfish 1, 2002
Performance Series
Inkjet print on paper
36 x 21 in.
Pages 88–89

Tracing The Decay of Fiction: Encounters with a Film by Pat O'Neill, 2002
Pat O'Neill, Rosemary Comella, Kristy H.A. Kang, and The Labyrinth Project, executive producer Marsha Kinder
Projected interactive DVD-ROM installation
Digital media, projectors, sound system, computers
Dimensions variable
Pages 190–91

Bamboo Action Map, 2003
Inkjet print on paper
87 x 46 in.
Pages 182–83

Bascom's Heart, 2003
Inkjet print on paper
22 x 26 in.
Page 92

Bill 'n Bob at the Lab, 2003
Inkjet print on paper
34 x 22 in.
Pages 52–53

Carpet 1, 2003
Inkjet print on paper
88 x 44 in.
Pages 184–85

Earfalls, 2003
Inkjet print on paper
26 x 22 in.
Page 129

Final Island, 2003
Performance Series (triptych)
Inkjet print on paper
48 x 42 in., 56 x 42 in., 44 x 42 in.
Pages 178–79

A Pair of Bones, 2003
Inkjet print on paper
46 x 54 in.
Page 35

Pupal Bingo, 2003
Inkjet print on paper
48 x 36 in.
Page 63

Snake is on the Right, 2003
Inkjet print on paper
82 x 46 in.
Pages 54–55

SD1, 2003
Inkjetprint on paper
23 x 43 in.
Page 95

SD3, 2003
Inkjet print on paper
23 x 43 in.
Page 94

Tiny Draws a Circle, 2003
Performance Series
Inkjet print on paper
82 x 46 in.
Pages 148–49

Untitled (Horn), 2003
Polyester laminate, horn, lacquer finish
21 x 5 x 5 in.
Page 47

The Contract, 2004
Inkjet print on paper
86 x 33 in.
Pages 142–43

Y Piso, 2004
Inkjet print on paper
78 x 46 in.
Page 93

ACKNOWLEDGMENTS

I am grateful to Pat O'Neill for his quiet determination to make art that is serious-minded without being arrogant, honest but not humorless, complex yet not impenetrable. His generosity in attending to all the tasks at hand in preparing this exhibition and catalogue will not be forgotten. What began as a professional relationship borne out of great respect for his talent has evolved into deepening personal friendships that are shared between Pat and Beverly O'Neill, my husband Kevin Sweeney, and myself.

Elsa Longhauser made a commitment to *Pat O'Neill: Views from Lookout Mountain* at a decisive moment in its development and has been the exhibition's closest ally and constant advocate. John Hanhardt's passion for independent artists is matched by the level of esteem he holds for their work—qualities that inform his interview with Pat O'Neill for this exhibition catalogue. John's high regard for Pat O'Neill's films led to their retrospective exhibition at the Solomon R. Guggenheim Museum in New York. In addition to her friendship over many years, I have been the fortunate recipient of Kathy Rae Huffman's genuine, good counsel. Like John, Kathy Rae is among a handful of curators whose long-time support of media artists and their endeavors have truly enhanced our global village. It was no small task for her to bring this exhibition to Manchester, England.

Everyone associated with *Pat O'Neill: Views from Lookout Mountain* is grateful to the funders enumerated below for their enthusiasm and support, particularly during such demanding political and stressful economic times as these: an anonymous donor; The Andy Warhol Foundation for the Visual Arts; The Kwon Family; The Labyrinth Project at the University of Southern California's Annenberg Center; and the Pasadena Art Alliance.

Joel Wachs is an impassioned arts advocate, contemporary art collector, and Director of The Andy Warhol Foundation for the Visual Arts. My respect for Joel's efforts on behalf of artists as well as his interest in safeguarding their free expression grows deeper with the passage of time. Pamela Clapp, Program Director of The Andy Warhol Foundation for the Visual Arts, has participated in two previous pivotal projects in my career: *Rolywholyover A Circus for museum by John Cage*, and *Uncommon Sense*, and has "gone to bat" again for this exhibition. Wonmi Kwon's kindness and continuing interest in art are very much appreciated. While they wish to remain anonymous, I respectfully acknowledge with gratitude an unusually modest and sensitive couple whose generous support has made producing this important document of Pat O'Neill's art a reality.

Heartfelt thanks go to the many dedicated individuals who are affiliated with the organizing and host museums for *Pat O'Neill: Views from Lookout Mountain*:

SANTA MONICA MUSEUM OF ART (ORGANIZING INSTITUTION)
The Santa Monica Museum of Art is grateful to the following foundations and organizations for general operating and specific project support: The Annenberg Foundation; the California Community Foundation; the City of Santa Monica Cultural/Arts Organizational Support Grant Program; the Good Works Foundation; and the Los Angeles County Arts Commission. Special thanks are due the Board of Trustees, the Friends and Members of the Santa Monica Museum of Art.

Board of Trustees: Laura Donnelley-Morton, Barbara J. Dunn, Dan Fauci, Charles Gaines, Carla Kirkeby, Kim McCarty, David Nochimson, V. Joy Simmons, M.D., Shidan Taslimi

Staff: Elsa Longhauser, Executive Director; Lisa Melandri, Deputy Director for Exhibitions and Programs; Christina Cassidy, Development Director; Alexandra Pollyea, Public Relations and Marketing Director; Asuka Hisa, Education Director; Christine Leahey, Visitor Services Director; Mary Weatherford, Finance Manager; Gretchen Gates, Registrar/Chief Preparator; and Denise Feathers-Dukoff, Executive Assistant.

CORNERHOUSE
Dave Moutrey, Director; Kathy Rae Huffman, Director of Visual Arts.

For his early support of my curatorial endeavors over the twenty-four years we worked together in New York and in Los Angeles, I am genuinely grateful to Richard Koshalek, President of Art Center College of Design. Under his dynamic directorship of The Museum of Contemporary Art, many hundreds of individuals were given the opportunity to take risks and to experiment in a sympathetic and fertile creative environment, including me.

John Bowsher, whose brilliant, unsung talents shined through the design of every exhibition at MOCA during his tenure there, once again provided sage advice about this exhibition's installation. Jang Park added his thoughtful guidance to the design as well. David Bradshaw's expertise helped to untangle and resolve many technological riddles. His positive spirit is always appreciated.

Stephanie Emerson, now head of the Los Angeles County Museum of Art's publications department, served as editor for several of my exhibition catalogues at MOCA. It was there that the foundation of our professional friendship was established. Once again, it has been a pleasure to experience the buoyancy of her intelligence and kindhearted working methods. In addition to exercising her very capable editing skills on behalf of this publication, Stephanie brought Pat O'Neill's work to the attention of Gerhard Steidl, who consequently became the book's printer and publisher. While he has built a unique shop of talented craftspeople, the key ingredient in Steidl's success is the personal care he affords to each book he shepherds through the production process. His "can do, will do" approach is inspiring.

I wish to extend my appreciation for the extra time, effort, ideas, and expertise of designer, Michael Worthington. In addition to his energetic shaping of this refined catalogue, he accepted my invitation to venture into collaboration with Pat O'Neill without a moment's hesitation. Pat and Michael have each drawn upon the other's talents to produce something I consider an artwork among the objects in the exhibition, one that resides in and circulates to the public though this book.

Pat O'Neill and I are both indebted to Paul Arthur, Howard Singerman, and Erika Suderburg for their beautifully written, thoughtful, illuminating essays; and to John Hanhardt for donating his time, energy and intelligence to the aforementioned interview. Josh White's clear-eyed, sensitive photographs of O'Neill's early collages and sculpture add to our understanding of his work. Meina Co's and Megan McGinley's contributions to the design process deserve to be recognized, as does Kevin Gralewski's professional interview transcriptions and swift delivery of the completed texts. Elizabeth Finch spent untold hours carefully honing the original Hanhardt/O'Neill interview into a clear, cohesive shape.

For their unwavering professional and personal friendship, I extend my warmest appreciation to: Sasha Anawalt; Remy Charlip, Tom Finkelpearl and Eugenie Tsai, Philip, Kitty and Ellen Finkelpearl, Ann Goldstein, Jackie Kain, Barbara London, Jonathan Rothbard, Elizabeth Streb and Laura Flanders, Ann Temkin, the memory of Ella King Torrey, Deborah Velders, David Wilson, Hirokazu Kosaka, and Brent Zerger. Heartfelt thanks are also offered for their gentle encouragement to Anne Bray, Linde Dehner and Bernd Wolk, Juan Devis and Laura Purdy, Tarlan Ghavami, Gai Gherardi, David James, Laurel Kishi, John W. Mazzola, Lauren Shenfield, Larry Stein and Patty Cogen, John Walsh, and Grahame Weinbren.

For their invaluable service to us in making this exhibition possible, Pat O'Neill and I wish to express our sincere appreciation to: the dedicated, hard-working team at the Santa Monica Museum, most particularly Lisa Melandri for her sensitive curatorial assistance and generous-spirited conduct in coordinating the most complex aspects of this project; Chris Cassidy for her enthusiastic and successful efforts to secure the funds necessary to fully realize this exhibition; Alexandra Pollyea for her alert, skillful communications with the press; Asuka Hisa for organizing unique programs that enhance the public's understanding of the artworks in the exhibition; Gretchen Gates for her creative, respectful approach to administering the installation of the art as well as to overseeing its safe transport to the museums participating the exhibition's tour; and Denise Feathers-Dukoff, Mary Weatherford and Christine Leahey all of whom provided effective and attentive support for our work on this project. For her dedicated assistance we thank Maria-Christina Villaseñor, Associate Curator of Film and Media Arts, Solomon R. Guggenheim Museum. We also thank MoCA Director, Jeremy Strick for loaning a 16mm projector to SMMoA; Christopher Cain for his generous, expert technical assistance; Rosemary Comella and Kristy H.A. Kang

for their elegant work; Finer Image Edition's staff, Rijan Shayani and Kristine Eubanks, for their high quality inkjet prints; DRG Enterprises for their excellent framing of the inkjet prints; JoAnn Hanley for her patient and conscientious coordination of the *Tracing The Decay of Fiction* installation; and Nancy Oppenheim for helping early on with press and promotion of the films especially for the premier of *The Decay of Fiction*.

Marsha Kinder's longtime friendship with the O'Neills and long-term support of Pat's career have been positively influential. For this exhibition she has obtained all of the necessary equipment as well as donated her staff's time and expertise to mount the installation of *Tracing The Decay of Fiction* in the best way possible.

Much more needs to be explored and written about how sound is deployed in Pat O'Neill's films. For now, because his contribution to all of O'Neill's completed 35mm films has been so profound, I wish to acknowledge the masterful talent of sound designer (and recently, director of photography), George Lockwood.

The primary lenders to this exhibition are Pat and Beverly O'Neill, and I am indebted to them for allowing such an extensive part of their collection to be on tour for two years. I sincerely appreciate David Rosenboom and Jacqueline Humbert's permission to circulate their treasured prints, and Gaby and Wilhelm Schuermann's agreeing to loan objects that they only recently acquired for the duration of the exhibition's tour.

Many more people than those who are singled out in these pages have contributed their time and energy to *Pat O'Neill: Views from Lookout Mountain* throughout the course of its journey to the public stage. I wish to commend them again here for their valuable support.

For their love and understanding, I give thanks to members of my immediate family: Al, Alex, Barbara, Edna, Harvey, Irwin, Jean, Jesse, Julianne, Kevin, Marilyn, Nina, Pablo, Paul, and Sarah.

—*Julie Lazar, Curator*

AUTHOR BIOGRAPHIES

Julie Lazar is an independent museum curator and consultant. She also serves as a curator for the New Media Department of KCET Public Television, and is currently producing a DVD-ROM with four companion books (designed by Dale Herigstad) based on the life and work of artist Remy Charlip. As a founding curator and later Director of Experimental Programs at The Museum of Contemporary Art, Los Angeles, she organized programs and exhibitions across all disciplines.

Paul Arthur is Professor of Literature and Film Studies at Montclair St. University. A regular contributor to *Film Comment* and *Cineaste* magazines, he is also coeditor *Millennium Film Journal*. His book on American avant-garde film, *A Line of Sight*, is forthcoming from the University of Minnesota Press.

Erika Suderburg is an artist and writer. Her work has been exhibited internationally including: the Pacific Film Archives, The Millennium Film Workshop, Capp Street Projects and The Museum of Modern Art. She is the co-editor of *Resolutions: Contemporary Video Practices* (1996) and the editor of *Space, Site, Intervention: Situating Installation Art* (2000) both published by the University of Minnesota Press.

Howard Singerman is Associate Professor of Art History at the University of Virginia and author most recently of *Art Subjects: Making Artists in the American University* (University of California Press, 1999). Over the past two decades, he has published on art in *Art in America, Artforum, Parkett, La Part de l'Oeil*, and *October*, and contributed to numerous exhibition catalogues, including *Mike Kelley: Catholic Tastes; Chris Burden: A Twenty-Year Survey*; and *A Forest of Signs: Art in the Crisis of Representation*. He has taught in the art history department at Barnard College and in a number of studio art departments and art schools, including UCLA, the California Institute of the Arts, and the Art Center College of Design.

John G. Hanhardt is Senior Curator of Film and Media Arts at the Solomon R. Guggenheim Museum of Art, New York.

PHOTO CREDITS

PART III

HANDLING IMPORTANT ASSIGNMENTS

~~It often seems that~~ *is found*
Sometimes the strength of a work lies in its accessibility through
~~diffípíe~~ *plan*
multiple routes of understanding. The original ~~program~~ for ~~its~~
construction discovery
structuring ~~may~~ lie beneath strata of accumulated decisions and
~~re-decisions~~ *repairs and recastings.* ⊛ The process of making ~~it/pore/possibilities~~ *contains* more *repeated*
possibilities than ~~that of preconception as it requires the~~ interaction
between the one
of sensibility and ~~pre-existing~~ ~~diagram~~ *reading itself* or image. The interaction may
proceed in any number of directions; The controlling discipline, *being*
is internal, ~~and~~ *It may be* only partly known. Once started, the process can
self-mutual dialogue(s)
accept any input, including unpredictabilities of technique, responses
and to
to other artists, living and dead, changes of season, location, and
conditions of life, ~~and so on.~~ Removals are as important as inclusions.
weaknesses
As a work begins to take shape ~~and a period of time passes~~, its ~~follies~~
become distinct from its virtues. Works ~~also~~ tend to divide or
combine ~~in a similar way~~— what may seem to be one piece may become
scene
~~two or more.~~ A ~~work~~ set aside last year for lack of cohesive
to another body of work
~~internal~~ connections may today become the germ of a new set of
~~decisions.~~ Its removal from one context releases it to generate a new
missing
one. Eventually, one leaves as many tracks as there are to be
~~found~~ around a waterhole in the desert.

The most difficult thing to do is to ... work at the time of starting, ... of the ... to today, weighs down ... another anything ... possibly be meaningful.

⁕ How to find the Chutzpah to ~~start~~ *begin* *again* against ~~amidst~~ the genuine possibility of disaster

⁕ It is to be desired that a ... If insights appear on more than one level of involvement simultaneously, the chances increase that the attempt will succeed.

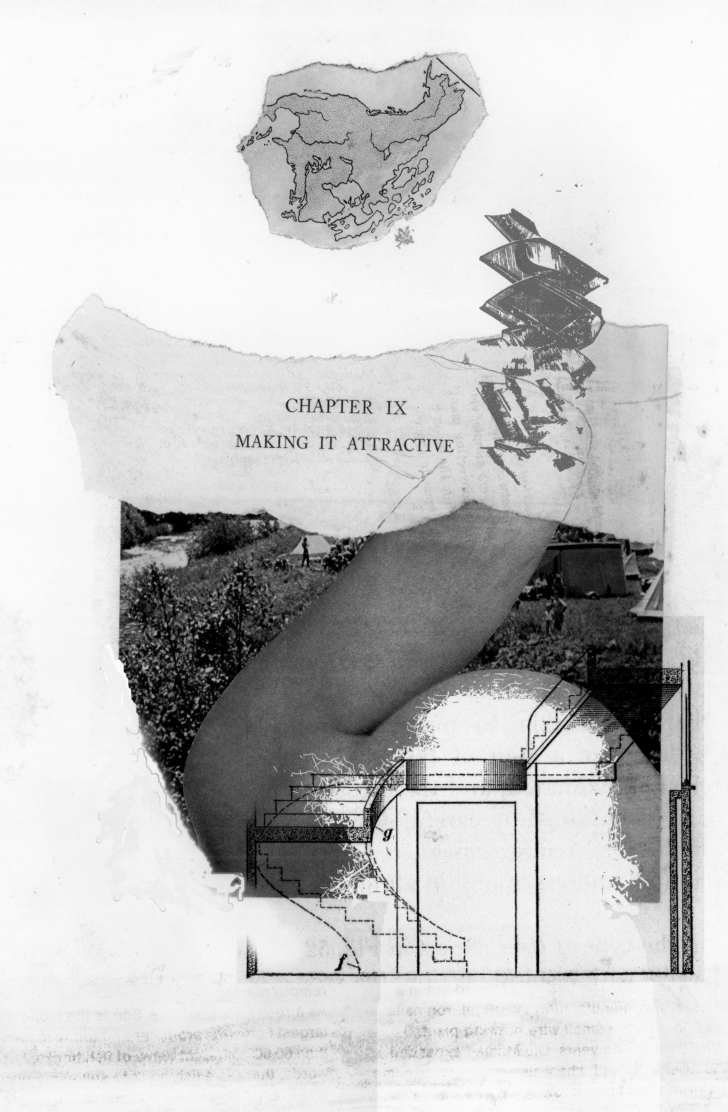

CHAPTER IX

MAKING IT ATTRACTIVE

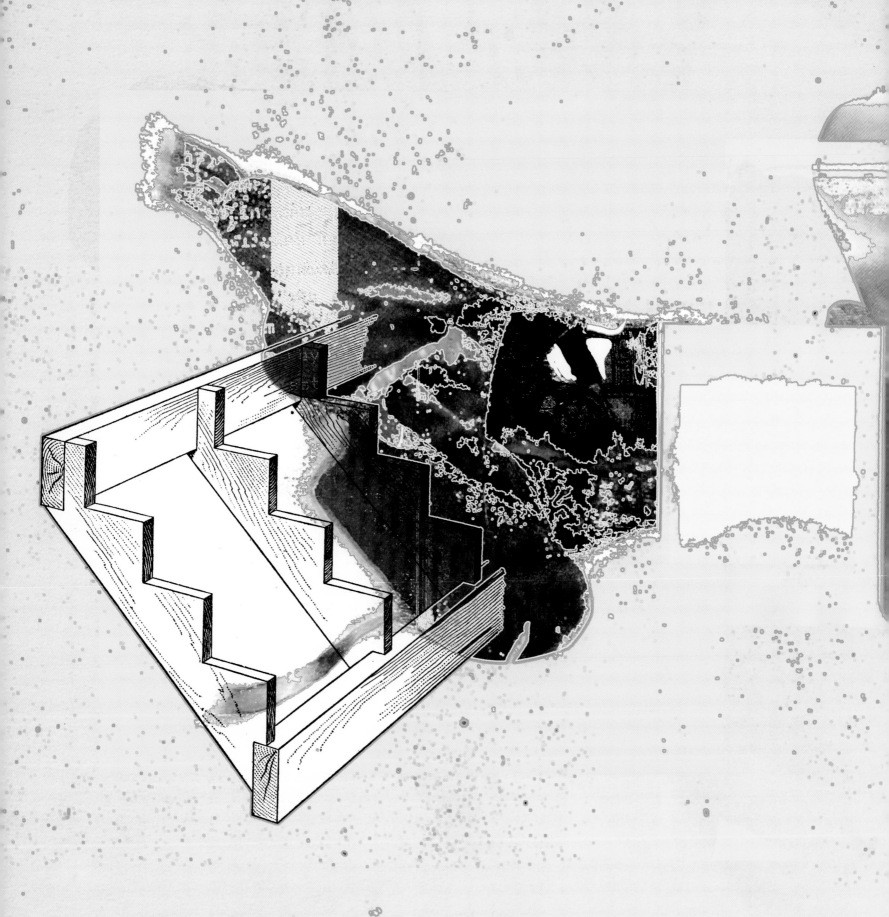

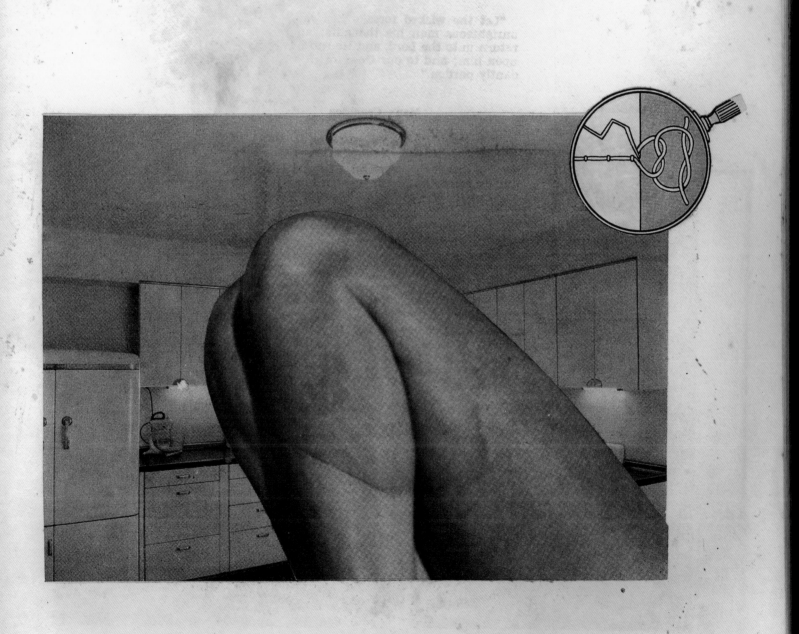